Vikings

The Most Badass Vikings in History

(A Captivating Guide to the Viking Age and Norse Mythology)

Shawn McKinney

Published By **Regina Loviusher**

Shawn McKinney

Vikings: The Most Badass Vikings in History (A Captivating Guide to the Viking Age and Norse Mythology)

ISBN 978-1-9992226-8-0

No part of this guidebook shall be reproduced in any form without permission in writing from the publisher except in the case of brief quotations embodied in critical articles or reviews.

Legal & Disclaimer

The information contained in this book is not designed to replace or take the place of any form of medicine or professional medical advice. The information in this book has been provided for educational & entertainment purposes only.

The information contained in this book has been compiled from sources deemed reliable, and it is accurate to the best of the Author's knowledge; however, the Author cannot guarantee its accuracy and validity and cannot be held liable for any errors or omissions. Changes are periodically made to this book. You must consult your doctor or get professional medical advice before using any of the suggested remedies, techniques, or information in this book.

Upon using the information contained in this book, you agree to hold harmless the Author from and against any damages, costs, and expenses, including any legal fees potentially resulting from the application of any of the information provided by this guide. This disclaimer applies to any damages or injury caused by the use and application, whether directly or indirectly, of any advice or information presented, whether for breach of contract, tort, negligence, personal injury, criminal intent, or under any other cause of action.

You agree to accept all risks of using the information presented inside this book. You need to consult a professional medical practitioner in order to ensure you are both able and healthy enough to participate in this program.

Table Of Contents

Chapter 1: The Viking Age

It is generally acknowledged that what has end up called the Viking Age lasted among the years of 800-1150 CE. During the ones 3 and a half of centuries of Viking growth and rule, extra than hundred thousand human beings of Scandinavian descent left their homelands to settle some vicinity else, with maximum of them finishing in Newfoundland, Greenland, Iceland, Ireland, England, Russia, Sicily, and France.

In France, the Viking humans have been capable of set up themselves most of the u . S . A .'s royalty with Gaange Rolf – or Rollo – being advanced to the number one ruler of Normandy, and and of the humans recognized nowadays because the Normans. Rollo is on occasion known as the primary Duke of Normandy - even though it modified into his son, William Longsword, and his grandson, Richard I, who first titled themselves "Count" and "Duke of Normandy" respectively.

It is an elevation that could proper away effects the English, who had completely prolonged records of preventing the Vikings. But, more on that later.

During the Viking Age, the Scandinavian human beings, because of their capability with boat-building, have been capable of sail to the Mediterranean, wherein they traded significantly with the Muslim world. Many Vikings additionally fought for the Byzantine emperors of Constantinople as mercenaries.

So, as you can see, Viking manner of life and characteristic an effect on grow to be extensive.

But, all matters have a place to begin, and the spread of the Viking global isn't always any exception. The starting point for the Viking Age is Lindisfarne, in any other case known as the Holy Island. A tidal island off the northeastern coast of England, Lindisfarne served as an essential part of Celtic Christianity courting decrease again to the sixth century.

A Northumbrian monastery modified into installation round 634 CE thru the use of Saint Aidan, an Irish monk sent from Iona thru King Oswald. Lindisfarne have end up the center of Christian evangelism in northern England and changed into amazing for some of of things, maximum particularly for what has grow to be known as the Lindisfarne Gospels – a famously illuminated manuscript of the Gospels of Matthew, Mark, Luke, and John.

Like many monasteries of the day, Lindisfarne emerge as a middle of high-quality wealth and treasure. Which probably make it masses tons less than sudden that the Vikings raided the monastery in 793 CE. It became the start of what we now recognise due to the fact the Viking Age, and it changed into a raid that brought on the fears at a few stage inside the English. That worry and anticipation of what was to go again have been recorded inside the Anglo-Saxon Chronicles.

"In this year fierce, foreboding omens got here over the land of the Northumbrians, and the wretched human beings shook; there were immoderate whirlwinds, lightning, and fiery dragons have been seen flying in the sky. These signs and signs and symptoms have been accompanied through first-rate famine, and a hint after the ones, that same 365 days on 6th ides of January, the ravaging of wretched heathen men destroyed God's church at Lindisfarne."

A Northumbrian scholar within the court docket docket docket of Charlemagne named Alcuin wrote in response to the raid on Lindisfarne:

"Never earlier than has such terror regarded in Britain as we've got now suffered from a pagan race ... The heathens poured out the blood of saints across the altar, and trampled at the our our bodies of saints in the temple of God, like dung inside the streets."

That grow to be a scene that performed out numerous times as England set up monasteries on many particular islands and peninsulas. Moreover, due to the format in their longships, that they'd a totally shallow draft, allowing them to flow into towards land than the ships of diverse countries – the Vikings were capable of excursion upriver and into shallower water which allowed them to raid and plunder less hard. Something they did quite regularly and pretty correctly.

And, no, the raid on Lindisfarne end up not accomplished with the aid of the usage of Ragnar Lodbrook as depicted at the History Channel's hit show Vikings. Even if Ragnar have been an actual ancient determine – an statement that is very a bargain dubious –

the recollections advised of him area his 365 days of start placed up-Lindisfarne.

Following the destruction and pillaging of Lindisfarne, the Viking raiders decrease again to England frequently, plundering monasteries for the gold and silver regularly stored there in addition to to seize slaves to supply home with them.

It became not lengthy earlier than the Vikings started out to remain in England in location of pass decrease again home after a a achievement raiding mission. At first, they set up wintry weather camps that might be broken come spring, allowing them to resume their buying and selling and raiding missions. Eventually, those winter camps transitioned into more everlasting settlements on lands they seized, which become specifically inside the north and east of England.

The Vikings conquered and controlled the Anglo-Saxon kingdoms of East Anglia,

Northumbria, and Mercia. They persevered to press south and to the west, threatening the dominion of Wessex and regarded poised to seize it as nicely until King Alfred the Great of Wessex rose up within the face of a fierce adversary.

In 865 CE, the Great Heathen Army, supposedly led with the beneficial useful resource of the sons of Ragnar Lodbrook, the Vikings rolled thru an entire lot of the u . S ., seizing lands and riches. Depending on whether or now not or no longer one believes the testimonies approximately the purpose for the invasion — the sons of Ragnar supposedly avenging his murder — there may be greater than sufficient number one source proof that the Great Heathen Army end up a real factor and united states of america after kingdom fell in advance than it.

Nevertheless, in 871 CE, Alfred of Wessex took control of his country, and he helped change the fortunes of England for the better. In 878 CE, King Alfred's forces dealt the Great Heathen Army led with the beneficial useful resource of Guthrum a blow with the beneficial resource of defeating them inside the Battle of Edington. The Treaty of Wedmore end up a end end end result of the struggle, and beneath terms of the treaty, Guthrum have end up pressured to transform to Christianity and became baptized at Aller in Somerset. Further, Guthrum and his army had been required to go away Wessex permanently and retire to their lands in East Anglia.

The revel in with Guthrum and the Great Heathen Army led Alfred to make a few reforms to his military and the defenses of his america to make it more difficult for raiding events to locate achievement. That did no longer forestall various Viking factions from stirring up problem and breaking the peace accords among Alfred and Guthrum – who had taken at the Christian call Athelstan at his baptism.

In 886, with some Viking combatants raiding and pillaging another time, Alfred defeated them and took the metropolis of London from them fast, fortifying it and stopping the Vikings from retaking the metropolis. In that equal 12 months, Alfred and Guthrum signed a treaty which partitioned England among them. The Viking territory, which comprised the east, northeast, and northwest, have grow to be referred to as the Danelaw, with Alfred being named king of the relaxation of the land.

In Danelaw territory, the people were project to Danish laws and punishments and had been capable of installation what they believed might be eternal settlements and allow them to put down their cultural roots. In 937 CE, despite the fact that, Alfred's grandson Athelstan defeated the Vikings on the Battle of Brunanburh and conquered the lands that comprised the Danelaw, making him England's first right king.

Although they misplaced the lands earned under the treaty amongst Guthrum and Alfred and the Danelaw emerge as no greater, that did not save you the fighting a number of the English and the Vikings, regardless of the reality that. Various Viking bands persisted to raid and plunder alongside the English coast for decades despite the fact that to include numerous rulers using precise techniques to try to save you the pillaging. For instance, in 991 CE, in some unspecified time in the future of the reign of King Aethelred, the Unready found his defenders defeated with the aid of a raiding birthday celebration led with the useful resource of way of Olaf Tryggvason and tried to pay him to prevent hostilities – a exercise called paying the Danegeld.

The Vikings persisted to have a presence in England, even having 4 kings of Viking historical past among 1013-1042 CE The maximum amazing of those 4 kings have become known as Cnut the Great – the King of Denmark and England. Cnut – a Christian himself – did no longer force the English to stick to Danish regulation. Instead, he dominated consistent with English regulation and customs. Cnut's closing intention come to be to create an empire that spanned the North Atlantic, joining Scandinavia and England collectively as one. However, after an extended infection, Cnut died at 39 years antique and in no way discovered out his dream – and neither need to his sons whose reigns have been all very brief and simply .

The very last recognized most critical Viking incursion into England got here inside the three hundred and sixty five days 1066 CE at the same time as Harald Hardrada, the King of Norway, and his military sailed up the Humber River and collectively with Tostig Godwinson – the brother of England's King

Harold Godwinson and Earl of Northumbria – marched on Stamford Bridge.

After a bloody warfare, King Hardrada, further to Tostig Godwinson, had been each killed, alongside side maximum of the Vikings warring parties. King Godwinson familiar a truce with the surviving combatants and allowed them to move away after they pledged no longer to attack England all over again. In what's probably genuinely an apocryphal story, the English victory modified into so entire that of the three hundred Viking ships that landed, survivors of the warfare wanted simply twenty-4 of them to leave.

Many historians bear in mind the struggle of Stamford Bridge signs the give up of the Viking Age. Several smaller raiding activities clashed with the English over again over the subsequent many years, but they did now not interact in huge scale warfare or attempts at settlement to any amount similarly.

However, in a single of these ironic twists of future that one regularly observes in history, King Harold Godwinson, fresh off his victory over the Vikings at Stamford Bridge, modified into forced to show his military and proper away march them south as William, the Duke of Normandy, landed in southern England, motive on invasion.

A little more than weeks later, William defeated King Harold's army on the Battle of Hastings. The Duke of Normandy's decisive victory at Hastings heralded the begin of the Norman conquest of England and William the Conqueror's ascension to the throne.

Normandy, if one recollects, is the northwestern part of France that modified into granted via Charles the Simple to Rollo inside the Treaty of Saint Clair sur Epte after his Viking warriors had besieged Paris. William the Conqueror, Duke of Normandy, changed into a proper away descendent of Rollo. The ironic twist said above is that with the Norman conquest of England complete in 1066 CE, the Vikings – or at the least, the direct descendants of the Vikings – assumed control of the whole u . S ., some element the English kings were in search of to stave off for masses of years.

Outside of England proper, the Vikings raided and pillaged monasteries alongside Ireland's northern and eastern coasts. By 840 CE, the Vikings started out to set up everlasting settlements and alternate routes throughout the whole of the Emerald Isle with the primary longphort – or a fortified port and searching for and selling middle – first being installed at what could in all likelihood emerge as called the city of Dublin. The Vikings went directly to installation longphorts in Cork, Limerick, Wexford, and Waterford – all but essential cities in Ireland nowadays.

The Vikings additionally set up sturdy footholds at the Isle of Man, the Shetlands, the Hebrides, the Faroe Islands, and the Orkney Islands. The Vikings installation earldoms and dominated over those locations, some of them becoming critical shopping for and selling centers of their very very personal proper. In lots of the ones places, even these days, feasible see the affects of the Vikings, speakme to the enduring legacy left behind.

Chapter 2: Notable Vikings

While there are plenty of superb Vikings via the ages, it's miles hard to surely buy into numerous those intended historical figures definitely due to the dearth of reliable number one sources. In fact, most of what we realise approximately a number of the ones Viking legends come from the sagas and poems produced ultimately of the day. It is made even greater dubious through the usage of way of the elements of the supernatural and mythical interwoven in the path of these poems and sagas.

For example, to fall back on History Channel's application all once more, the names Ragnar Lodbrook, Ivar the Boneless, Bjorn Ironside, and Aslaug, among others, were forged into the spotlight. And even as they deal with them as real historic figures and legendary Viking heroes, the truth of the problem is that tons of what we understand approximately they all has been gleaned from mythological writings

interwoven with supernatural factors —
assets much like the numerous sagas in
conjunction with the Tales of Ragnar's Sons.

Some historians accept as true with Ragnar
himself is actually an amalgamation of
numerous Viking heroes combined to make
a legend. His spouse, Aslaug's, very very
own information is doubtful at high-quality,
given her mythical parentage. Moreover, we
do no longer recognize for pleasant that Ivar
the Boneless is an real historic determine or,
like his meant father Ragnar, definitely an
amalgamation of various characters in those
sagas.

Bjorn, rather, does have a prolonged
ancient report from an entire lot of
particular property, which appears to
installation him as an actual and credible
ancient discern. Nevertheless, he have
become no longer named the son of Ragnar
Lodbrook till it modified into penned inside
the thirteenth century in the Tales of
Ragnar's Sons.

Despite that, although, the document and proof amassed through the years shows Bjorn to be an real ancient decide. Bjorn is mentioned in Frankish sources Annales Bertiniani and Chronicon Fontanellense as taking difficulty in a siege and plundering of Paris across the latest 12 months in 856-857 CE. It modified into written that Bjorn constructed a fortification at the island of Oissel, that is above Rouen in Normandy – a base of operations he held onto for years.

There is some hypothesis that Bjorn took factor in the expeditions to the Mediterranean, however there's no ancient evidence to again up that assertion. What we realize comes from Frankish and Arab property that factor out a big Viking raid into the area someday amongst 859-861, making it feasible, however no longer a extraordinary element with the useful resource of using any manner. Bjorn is likewise credited with being the founder of the Munsö Dynasty, who ruled Sweden at some point across the 9th century. Although the ancient file does replicate the Munsö Dynasty being actual, the evidence that Bjorn became the progenitor of the dynasty is sketchy – at excellent.

Our maximum dependable belongings come from non-Scandinavian belongings which consist of the Anglo-Saxon Chronicles, the Fragmentary Annals of Ireland, and Annales Bertiniani and Chronicon Fontanellense. And, in element because of the ones assets, we do have a prolonged record that information the exploits of some very famous Vikings who've left a huge footprint on records.

Erik the Red is a acquainted name that is stated quite regularly at the same time as discussing the greater well-known Vikings. He have end up an explorer and adventurer who got here from a circle of relatives with a statistics of inflicting problem. According to the Iceland Saga, Erik the Red's father, Thorvald Asvaldsson, were banished from

Norway after "some killings" and traveled to Iceland, which, with the aid of that factor, had been substantially settled. It is believed that Erik were about ten on the time.

However, around the 12 months 982 CE, years after his father's loss of life, Erik the Red, now thirty- years antique, became banished from Iceland for three years after killing Eyiolf the Foul over a dispute approximately some of his father's possessions that he had traveled lower back to Iceland to acquire — devices his father had delivered with him from Norway. That set into movement a sequence of activities that cemented Erik the Red's region in information.

Although most well-known historic bills credit score score Erik the Red with having decided Greenland, the historical document shows that became a protracted way from the truth. The Icelandic Sagas credit Gunnbjorn Ulfsson with the discovery of Greenland — sighting the landmass nearly a hundred years earlier than Erik the Red. After Gunnbjorn sighted Greenland, Snaebjorn Galti visited Greenland and tried to establish settlements - settlements that in the long run failed miserably.

Though he did now not discover it, Erik the Red did set up the primary eternal agreement on Greenland. It modified into in the path of his three years spent in exile from Iceland that he first commenced exploring and number one made his manner to Greenland. When his term of exile grow to be up, Erik returned to Iceland and started out to rally guide for a eternal agreement, promising greater favorable residing situations than that that they had on Iceland.

Erik's earnings pitch worked as he left Iceland with a huge quantity of Icelanders advantageous for a modern day life in Greenland. They set up colonies on the southwest coast – the eastern agreement, which is in contemporary-day Qaqortoq, and the western agreement in modern-day-day Nuuk.

Despite flourishing over nearly five hundred years, in the end, the Little Ice Age, pirate raids, conflicts with the Inuit, and the abandonment thru the usage of Norway blended to bring about the decline of the settlements in Norway — in spite of the reality that lines of them continue to be even in recent times.

Perhaps the most famous Viking of all, although, is the son of Erik the Red — Leif Erikson. Likely born in Iceland in the end among 970-980 CE, Leif had an adventurer's spirit from the begin. He and his group traveled to Norway in 999 CE, wherein Leif have end up a hirdman — a member of the king's armed companions — of King Olaf Tryggvason. With Norway within the approach of converting from the vintage religion to Christianity, Leif himself have become a convert and have end up charged with the venture of introducing Christianity to Greenland.

According to bills of the time, Leif have become blown off course on his way to Greenland and observed land to the west. Contemporary money owed united states that it was a provider issuer named Bjarni Herjolfsson, who first sighted the landmass even though he did no longer make landfall. It have become Leif, who had reportedly mustered a crew after he provided Bjarni's deliver and headed towards those new lands – which offers the supply of his enduring fame.

As related within the Saga of Erik the Red, Leif's discovery turn out to be portrayed as such:

"After being tossed approximately at sea for a long term, he chanced upon land in which he had not expected any to be determined. Fields of self-sown wheat and vines were growing there; additionally, there have been timber known as maple, and that they took specimens of all of them. Leif moreover chanced upon guys clinging to a deliver's smash, whom he introduced home and decided secure haven for over the wintry weather. In so doing he confirmed his strong person and kindness. (...) Afterward, he have become called Leif the Lucky."

Leif and his group had been the primary Europeans to set foot on the land that might grow to be North America. Thanks to the bounty of grape vines they decided within the location, Leif named the land that that they'd decided Vinland (Wine Land). Vinland end up believed to embody the location from the Strait of Belle Isle in Newfoundland to the Gulf of St. Lawrence, to Prince Edward Island, and Brunswick.

Almost five hundred years earlier than Christopher Columbus supposedly "determined what may emerge as America," Leif Erikson landed in, "a rocky and desolate area he named Helluland (Flat-Rock Land;

possibly Baffin Island). After venturing similarly through sea, he landed the second time in a forested region he named Markland (Forest Land; in all likelihood Labrador). Finally, after greater days at sea, he landed in a verdant vicinity with a mild climate and massive sources of salmon. As winter approached, he decided to encamp there and broke his birthday party into organizations – one to stay at camp and the opportunity to discover the u . S . A .."

These are a handful of Viking leaders who left the maximum critical imprint on information. Again, what we understand of these mythical figures come typically from sources not of Scandinavian basis, because the written records of the Vikings is sparse. Most of their histories come inside the form of sagas and poems that cannot be taken at face fee, nor relied upon as an accurate accounting of the ancient file.

Chapter 3: Reasons For Viking Expansion

The 3 to 4 hundred years that marked the Viking Age observed the satisfactory increase in their human beings and their way of lifestyles. Before the cease of the 8th century, the Scandinavian humans were especially a way of life of agriculture and fishing. They have been an insular folks who did not have hundreds inside the manner of touch with the area at big.

However, that every one changed thru the usage of the give up of the 8th century, with most people the use of the raid on Lindisfarne because the location to begin of sweeping adjustments within the Scandinavian people and their way of life – adjustments that might all of the time modify them and the route of information.

But the question is, why did the Vikings abandon their insular procedures and begin increasing their reach to start with?

That trouble is one which has generated pretty a bit of debate among college students. There are numerous thoughtful theories about why the Vikings broadened their horizons during the Viking Age. Each of them simply as viable and legitimate because of the truth the ultimate. It is a query that has now not but been answered with any reality – and likely in no way will, given the shortage of number one belongings from the Scandinavians themselves.

One of the posited theories has to do with the populace and the demographics of Scandinavia. More specially, one department of this argument believes that overpopulation of Scandinavia introduced about the human beings seeking out new, uninhabited – or at least, much less inhabited – land to construct their houses and farms on.

The concept rests at the perception that actually earlier than the start of the Viking age, Scandinavia professional a population boom, and for the motive that appropriate land modified right into a finite useful aid within the vicinity, topics had been given uncomfortably crowded for the populace.

A modern-day, Frankish cleric, named Dudo of Normandy, inform us that the populace growth befell way to the wildly promiscuous strategies of the Vikings. Dudo claimed the Vikings engaged in, "shameless and illegal intercourse to breed innumerable progeny."

In his ebook, A History of the Vikings, Welsh student and creator Gwyn Jones echoed the idea first posited via Dudo — even though from a more instructional, in choice to judgmental point of view. Jones wrote about the exercise of polygamy the diverse Vikings, not as an immoral workout, however one of the regular Scandinavian norms at the time. "Great guys had wives with the resource of marriage-agreement and, in the event that they wished, by the usage of manner of unfastened-bridal. For any, save the very awful, a quiverful of sons emerge as welcome. They had been proof of someone's virility. A quiverful of sons would probably, of route, need to be furnished for, and this could have located awesome stress on chieftains and farmers, in phrases of providing suited enough assets to their sons."

As biased as Dudo's disapproving view is, it's far difficult to bargain the concept that the populace led the Vikings to appearance outdoor their everyday borders for a domestic. The belief among a few historians is that the increasing population of Scandinavian lands left many with out property or reputation. And probably greater importantly, due to the fact the form of humans endured to upward thrust, their opportunities for obtaining each decreased sharply.

With such plenty of fellows having a quiverful – or greater – of sons strolling round and desiring to inherit land to keep the circle of relatives lineage, it isn't unexpected to recognize that land ultimately fell into short deliver.

Running alongside the traces of the demographic model but final on the fringes, is the idea that it come to be no longer land that ran short usually, but girls. There is a college of concept available who endorse that because of the fact tremendous Norse tribes engaged within the exercise of female infanticide – that is, the killing of newborn lady infants because it changed into sons who perpetuated the family line – there has been a lack of women who can also want to undergo more sons to the Viking guys. Thus, the Vikings began to extend their reap clearly to find out new substances of fertile ladies who need to provide them with a "quiverful of sons."

James Barrett is the deputy director of Cambridge University's McDonald Institute for Archaeological Research and is a proponent of that principle, as he said in a

2008 interview with Discovery News. "Selective girl infanticide have end up recorded as a part of pagan Scandinavian exercising in later medieval sources, collectively with the Icelandic sagas." Although, he come to be careful to qualify his assertion as certainly one concept among many. "It is tough to recognize in the archaeological report, so the declare have to remain a hypothesis."

The overpopulation principle is one that deserves attention, however it is also tough to reveal one manner or the other. Nevertheless, the concept that the exercise of woman infanticide contributed to Norse increase in some unspecified time in the future of the Viking age has even an entire lot less evidence to useful resource it.

Another precept for the spread of the Vikings is a extra pragmatic one, and that concept is straightforward — economics. With more facilities of wealth being mounted now not first-class in mainland

Europe but with the upward thrust of the Islamic global, wealth changed into developing round the sector. Trade routes had been increasing, with some of them shifting northward and stepping into touch with the Viking people.

Naturally, as many others have been drawn to those growing facilities of wealth during Europe and for the duration of the Mediterranean, the Vikings desired to get their sincere percent. As such, the ones facilities of wealth were often targeted through using the Vikings who raided and plundered for the silver and gold.

That principle gained a few legs with the discovery of more than one Viking hoards of wealth. In precise, the Cuerdale Hoard, found in 1840 in Lancashire, England, and contained extra than 8,six hundred quantities of silver coins as well as silver English and Carolingian earrings. In 2007, each different Viking hoard have become exposed close to the town of Harrogate in

North Yorkshire in England. The Vale of York Hoard or Harrogate Hoard, as it has been called, contained 617 silver coins and extra than sixty 5 different treasured items.

Eventually, even though, the raiders grew to come to be traders due to the fact the Vikings started out out putting in area centers of exchange in their very very own, with an eye constant consistent toward profiting from the growing financial system of the ever-developing global. Famously, the Vikings hooked up fortified towns or longphorts in Ireland – Cork, Dublin, and Limerick, amongst others. Historians furthermore make a phrase of Viking trading centers in England, France, or maybe inside the Mediterranean place.

Piggybacking on the monetary idea is one posited by way of way of a few historians that honor and looting changed into but a few different reason for Viking growth. According to a few college students who reference literary and archaeological evidence together with the scaldic poems and rune stones, many Vikings launched raiding expeditions as a way to boost their very own esteem further to growth their personal fortunes – a principle reinforced by using the discovery of silver hoards in Cuerdale and Harrogate.

The honor and loot idea is probably one that might have appealed to the later sons of massive households. It might allow them to attain both the repute and wealth they will not be capable of gain had they remained of their fatherland. Striking out on their very own could probably permit them to assemble a name and a fortune for themselves.

Though possibly not the number one the use of pressure for increase at a few stage in the Viking Age, the historical and archaeological proof that has been unearthed in various places may seem to expose that smooth economics at least carried out a huge feature. As they say — comply with the cash.

Though no longer always a famous principle — and a specifically modern one — is the most effective posed with the resource of using students which consist of British historian and Professor of Medieval History at Westfield College on the University of London Henry R. Loyn.

Professor Loyn piggybacked on the overpopulation idea and brought his belief that climate trade exacerbated the hassle, which introduced about Scandinavians searching out new lands that have been more hospitable. He notes that even though the Viking Age was a warm, dry length sooner or later of Europe as an entire, Scandinavia skilled an surprisingly bitter bloodless spell a number of the years of 860-940 CE — a crucial duration of Viking agreement in England.

Loyn posits that the bloodless spell skilled over those sixty years made a harsh dwelling surroundings even more hard and averted the Vikings from farming their lands and feeding their people. Those situations might also additionally properly have been sizable inside the initial segment of Viking increase and colonization of the British Islands in addition to one-of-a-kind islands within the North Atlantic.

Many historians furthermore keep in mind that politics — each inner and external — done an vital function in Viking boom and colonization of overseas lands. Some of those historians describe the outside political problems that precipitated the Vikings colonization efforts due to the fact the "pull factors."

These college students argue that the shortage of any form of centralized authorities and the division of the lands into smaller, a good buy less prepared, and further tribal "kingdoms," is what "pulled" the Vikings to them. Smaller, bite-sized "kingdoms" similar to those of Northumbria, Wessex, Mercia, East Anglia, Essex, Kent, and Sussex with out a centralized and unified authorities or military protection were much less complicated to select out off and triumph over for colonization and agreement.

Add to that the internal political problems — what the ones college students communicate over with due to the fact the "push factors" — like instability inner their private homelands. Just in advance than the Viking Age, there has been mass political instability internal Scandinavia as a push for additonal centralized governments in lands previously ruled with the useful resource of chieftains or jarls had been slowly however inexorably shifting closer to the contemporary-day international locations of Norway, Sweden, and Denmark.

With the smaller petty kingdoms have been being eaten up and disbanded via powerful kings as they sought to set up dynastic manipulate of those burgeoning international locations, those once powerful chieftains have been driven out (or simply killed) and sought shelter some vicinity else. That mass exodus of these chieftains triggered them touchdown in remote places lands like western Europe and the British Isles, in search of to installation a electricity base in their very personal.

Expounding upon the concept that Viking chieftains and others fled their nearby lands as powerful kings commenced out consolidating and centralizing their energy is the tale of Norway's King Harald Sigurdsson as relayed in Icelandic historian, poet, and baby-kisser Snorri Sturluson's Heimskringla – a historic account of Norwegian kings.

King Harald compelled his way to the throne and earned a recognition for brutality – and some of nicknames that pondered that. The most commonplace has been translated as Harald the Ruthless or Harald Hardrada (tough ruler). As relayed in Sturluson's Heimkringla, King Harald took a tough line towards farmers who refused to pay their taxes and supported Harald's enemies ultimately of a rebel.

"So the king had the farmers seized; some of them he ordered to be maimed, others killed, and maximum of them deprived of all their possessions. All individuals who may additionally additionally want to interrupt out fled."

It have to appear that this faculty of concept, that the Viking Age growth is the quit give up end result of an remarkable storm. Political instability in different European global locations because of the shortage of a centralized government made it easier for the Vikings to flee lands in the middle of their very own political instability as more centralized governments were beginning to shape, made it less complicated for the Vikings to overcome and settle in lands at a few degree inside the era of their most first-rate increase.

Furthermore, like one-of-a-kind theories, this one has a few legs and might be some other component inside the enlargement of Viking settlements out of doors Scandinavia.

Yet every other idea approximately Viking growth not fine touches a sensitive trouble that has derailed many a own family meal but grabs hold of it with each hands – faith. Historians Rudolf Simek and Bruno Dumezil have written extensively approximately the Viking raids and expansion being direct retaliation for Emperor Charlemagne's wars in the direction of the pagans. Professor Simek is on file as announcing, "it isn't always a twist of fate if the early Viking hobby happened at a few stage in the reign of Charlemagne."

As Christianity spread further north, using deep into Scandinavian lands, those burgeoning international locations – most of whom had started to discover as Christian global places thru manner of the quit of the Viking Age – developed deep rifts the numerous population as some embraced the modern-day religion even as others clung to their vintage ideals. The exodus of people from Scandinavian lands turn out to be helped along through some fleeing spiritual persecution because the modern day order became set up, and that they sought out lands wherein they will exercise their very very own traditional faith.

Some historians additionally consider the Viking attacks and pillaging of non secular centers in England and a few different place modified into direct retaliation for the invasion of Christian missionaries into their homelands. It is hard to quantify that belief with a few factor within the historic record, but it's also a idea that can not be dismissed definitely out of hand.

Although, it does appear more logical and, therefore more likely that monasteries and extraordinary religious facilities had been targeted in reality for the wealth they contained. The one counter-argument is to impeach how the Viking raiders must have acknowledged about the big wealth that changed into saved at religious facilities in the course of Christendom earlier than they sacked and pillaged Lindisfarne.

Still, the changing landscape of faith in Scandinavia ought to thoroughly have performed a function in Viking boom.

Furthermore, of path, the quality solution to the query of why the Vikings began out to extend in the first vicinity became because they could. Always highly professional boat builders, the Vikings made some technological advances that allowed them to look properly past their traditional crusing lanes and into lands in no way dreamed of a era in advance than.

By the time of the Viking Age, boat constructing generation had superior to the issue that Norse longships – small, fast, and lethal – ruled the seas. Viking shipbuilders had determined to create a watertight shell via first laying the keel and stem. After that, they would lay masking planks, every one riveted to the subsequent, that is referred to as the lapstrake approach. Internal ribbing, laid internal of the planking, delivered more balance and electricity to the hull of the boat. The Viking longships have been so technologically advanced for their time that it end up now not prolonged in advance than all ships have been constructed like this in some unspecified time in the future of Northern Europe.

In his ebook, Vikings: The North Atlantic Saga, archaeologist and anthropologist William W. Fitzhugh, director of the Smithsonian's Arctic Studies and a senior scientist at the National Museum of Natural History defined some of the features and outcomes of Viking shipbuilding.

"The addition of oars and sails gave Viking boats an advantage over all extraordinary watercraft in their day in tempo, shallow draft, weight, capacity, maneuverability, and seaworthiness. Viking boats had been designed to be dragged at some stage in lengthy portages in addition to to stand up to fierce ocean storms. Such ships gave the Vikings the capability to change, make conflict, deliver animals, and pass open oceans and, on the equal time, furnished sufficient protection and protection for the group."

The Vikings, in search of to innovate and make bigger their reap even in addition, decided that via which include huge sails to their ships, they will probable journey even farther — a reality reinforced with the resource of using their advantage deep into the Mediterranean sooner or later of the Viking Age.

Not pretty, there can be no real consensus among scholars and historians about what sparked the mass migration at a few degree inside the Viking Age. There seems to be validity in nearly every principle proposed, that may appear to make it likelier than not that it have turn out to be a aggregate of these reasons that fueled the increasing reach of the Norse in the direction of the Viking Age.

Chapter 4: Viking Culture

Despite depictions of the Vikings as a lawless, barbaric, nearly anarchist society, the truth is pretty specific. Culture in Scandinavia modified into quite orderly with society constructed into terrific training.

One vital distinction must be made at this element. So a protracted way, we've got got used "Vikings" and "Scandinavians" interchangeably. However, there can be a pointy line of division that desires to be understood. Although all Vikings had been Scandinavian in starting location, no longer all Scandinavians have been taken into consideration Vikings.

The term Viking refers at the entire to folks who took to the sea, who plundered, looted, and invaded overseas lands. The term Viking itself, whose beginning is the hassle of masses scholarly debate, turn out to be used normally with the resource of the usage of English and some Frankish writers however have become now not without difficulty utilized by Scandinavians to refer to themselves.

Some college students don't forget that the phrase Viking comes from the antique Norse word vik, which refers to a small inlet or cove – a small fjord from which raiders must launch attacks on provider enterprise ships. Henry Sweet, a philologist who specialized in Germanic languages which incorporates Old English and Old Norse, argued that the phrase Viking is in reality Old Norse for "pirate." British historian and influential professor Peter Sawyer stated the word Viking refers to a specific region of Viken, alongside the Oslo Fjord.

"This district became of outstanding fee for it modified into there that the Danes should advantage the iron that have end up produced in Norway. If, as appears in all likelihood, the phrase Viking before the whole lot cited the populace of Viken, it can provide an cause behind why the English, and splendid they, called Scandinavian pirates Vikings, for England grow to be the natural objective for men from Viken who selected exile as raiders."

Although the word "Viking" does appear on some Scandinavian rune stones, it's miles used extra like an outline or a verb in vicinity of a fine set of human beings. The ancient file indicates it's miles more likely some said themselves as Ostmen or Austmann. And distinctive cultures said them in special techniques as nicely. Scholars point out that Scandinavian buyers had been normally called Norsemen – or Northmen – or each different time period that highlighted their beginning.

Sawyer is going on to aspect out, "The Irish records call them pagans or in reality foreigners, the French referred to as them Northmen, the Slavs referred to as them the Rus (which gave Russia its call), and the Germans knew them as Ashmen in connection with their use of ash wooden for their boats."

The scholarly debate maintains to in the intervening time, and we appear as not going to attain at a definitive answer as we are to get one about the motivations for the Scandinavian human beings to increase and settle in different lands. The detail is truly this — the Vikings made up a small percentage of the Scandinavian people, however they have been nonetheless a vital thing of the way of life as an entire.

The subculture of Scandinavians — and the Vikings — changed into tightly primarily based into three degrees. Jarls, who've been basically petty kings or aristocracy. Karls, who made up the lower training — smiths, investors, farmers, or even the Vikings. The 1/3 elegance became the thralls or slaves. Slavery become a extensive exercise in the direction of Scandinavia, making a few pupils lend extra credence to the idea that getting new slaves had been the number one cause pressure of Viking tours into foreign lands. That may be a thing in the ones tours but is not probable the primary purpose pressure.

But let us start the talk with the thralls, of which there have been sorts. The first changed into the bondsman – any man or woman who couldn't pay a debt and become obligated to art work it off. Once one paid off their debt, they had been freed. The second changed into the slave, any person taken during a raid and pressured to art work their captor. Slaves had absolutely no rights, however consistent with a few students, they will buy their freedom. Slaves have been essential to walking a farm and, therefore, to the Scandinavian economic system as an entire.

Paupers and vagrants – the horrible and unlucky, folks that did no longer have their personal domestic – had been often taken into consideration to be at the identical societal level as thralls. Although they were freemen, they did not enjoy the equal whole slate rights as others. For example, in

Iceland, a pauper have become not allowed to marry. So even as it changed into now not pretty the stigma of being a thrall, there have been though effects for being awful.

The next on the social ladder in Viking way of life modified into the Karls. The majority of the people in Scandinavia made up this magnificence – the freemen and landowners. However, even this splendor carried precise layers inner it. Among the Karls were community chieftains – frequently the wealthiest guys with the most vital tracts of land. The freemen supported the community chieftains inside their small sphere of have an impact on, but when they misplaced the useful useful resource in their freemen, they regularly misplaced their jobs – if not their lives – along with it.

Merchants moreover helped populate the Karl elegance. The shoppers most often did not have their very very personal lands, however they cherished all the rights of freemen. Many freemen did not have lands of their very own due to the lack of to be had land. Most labored as fishermen and farmhands, and some of them have been tenant farmers.

The 0.33 tier of Scandinavian way of lifestyles become the Jarls – the petty kings who've been widely talking rulers of a selected vicinity. Unlike one of a kind European global locations, the Norse human beings did not view the Jarls with a few aspect close to the same reverence. They were maximum genuinely now not the god-like figures some Kings have been supposed to be.

The name of Jarl may be a hereditary perceive or one which end up surpassed alongside through the usage of manner of some other, however it changed into a title predicted to be held thru the strongest and maximum succesful fighter in a place. Unlike Kings, Jarls have been expected to combat along their human beings. He turned into imagined to be an splendid military chief, formidable, modern, and inspirational.

The call of Jarl may be out of area virtually as with out issues as it could take delivery of. Moreover, now not like international places like England or France, a member of the lower magnificence – the Karls – may want to ascend to the higher position of Jarl. There have become upward mobility in Scandinavian way of existence that did now not exist in special European global locations.

One may probably in no way partner Viking manner of lifestyles with modern-day-day establishments of democracy. Nevertheless, greater students in recent times are doing really that. Rather than the lawless and brutally violent society, the Vikings are regularly depicted as having, Scandinavian life-style end up starkly precise. At normal durations, they could keep a large assembly referred to as the Thing.

The ancient document – particularly that of Norway's Law of the Gulathing – indicates that all loose men who have been of age may also want to take part in a Thing, which turn out to be held at a close-by, nearby, or supra-nearby degree and functioned as each a parliament and a court docket docket. The characteristic of the Things modified into to locate resolutions to a dispute but also to legislate and make political choices and choose leaders - a pick – and a king.

Scholars in recent times accept as true with that the Scandinavian Things helped lay the muse for present day day democratic institutions insomuch as it is an elected body meeting with the idea of neutrality, equality, and representing the interests of a huge type of humans. Some students argue that Things have been most usually dominated by manner of the wealthiest human beings of a network who carried the most effect. However, others assert that any free man, no matter wealth or recognition, modified into capable of placed forth his case for talk and arbitration.

Things changed, regardless of the reality that, due to the fact the Viking Age got here to a near even as national Kings emerged and began out consolidating their energy, keeping it for themselves in place of letting all and sundry have a say. By the later Middle Ages, the power and effect of Things were absolutely long gone, and they in reality functioned as courts that met to treatment disputes rather than represent the hobbies of the humans.

While maximum Scandinavians are depicted as Viking warriors, it overlooks the truth that that they had a extraordinary amount of proficient human beings – artists and artisans, musicians, jewelers, painters, and so forth. Scandinavian paintings turn out to be drastically considered to be great artwork, and as they increased their presence inside the worldwide, it changed into artwork that got here to be coveted via many. The majority of Scandinavians had been surely farmers or fishermen. But there were moreover blacksmiths, brewers, weavers, carpenters, and lots of different professional craftsmen. Their art work with amber, the usage of it to make earrings, was a few factor that have turn out to be coveted via the ones in the Roman and Byzantine empires. Simply placed, the Scandinavians had been not without a doubt one-trick ponies.

Viking way of life became moreover a way of lifestyles that enjoyed their enjoyment time as hundreds as anybody. They were said to revel in gambling sports sports activities — things like mock fight and wrestling. They loved mountaineering, swimming, and aggressive javelin throwing. Scandinavians cherished a place activity Knattliek, which is perception to be much like hockey. They moreover enjoyed board video games further to an terrific chess match. The photograph of Viking human beings sitting down for a board recreation seems in fact at odds with the forever dour photo of them we gather in pop culture.

Another image that doesn't in form what we are commonly shown these days is that of the wild, dirty, dust-caked, and blood-soaked warrior. In reality, the Scandinavian people placed a top magnificence on grooming and hygiene. Once their exchange routes accelerated, investors and jarls regularly wore silks and great cloaks. Their hair emerge as smartly braided, and that they wore tremendous, intricately crafted necklaces similarly to arm and wristbands.

Cleanliness some of the Scandinavian people changed into one signal of the wealth and status of someone. Nevertheless, greater than that, nicely grooming also carried a non secular significance. Adherents of the antique faith believed wholeheartedly in Ragnarok — the prevent of the vintage global and the emergence of the today's. According to the spiritual way of life, whilst Ragnarok comes, there may be a remarkable conflict an excellent way to cause the lack of life of some of the antique gods. The ship Naglfar is concept to were made without a doubt out of the fingernails and toenails of the useless. The ship will ferry a big quantity of people to participate in the final battle with the gods.

Scandinavians possibly stored their nails trimmed genuinely to offer the materials to construct the deliver.

"Well-groomed and smooth" does no longer quite mesh with the wild-eyed, filthy, ax-wielding, crazed warrior image from maximum pop-cultural depictions in recent times.

Chapter 5: Women In Viking Society

Viking Age society became similar to precise European cultures of the day – in maximum cases male-orientated and dominated. For the maximum issue, the Scandinavians held to traditional gender roles – men did the looking, cooking, and farming, whilst their ladies cared for the residence and raised the kids. The burial mounds determined by means of archaeologists spotlight traditional gender roles a number of the Scandinavians – guys have been normally buried with guns and tool even as women were buried with family gadgets, their needlework, and jewellery.

Like most in their contemporaries, the existence of a woman in Viking society turned into targeted round the residence and rearing the youngsters. They had been basically housewives, however at the equal time as their husbands have been called far from home, the opposite halves had the duty of going for walks the family farm, every bit as organisation as their husbands.

However, there have been precise strains of demarcation among girls in Viking society in preference to women in traditional European society that set them apart from each other.

In Viking Age Scandinavia, ladies had a diploma of freedom that girls in conventional European society need to have in no way conceived of. Women should personal belongings and have their non-public corporations. Although marriages were however organized and negotiated with the useful resource of the male head of her family – typically while she modified into among twelve and fifteen – a woman want to call for a divorce. All she may want to do have become name witnesses to her home and marriage mattress and claim her goal to divorce her husband, and it become achieved. Moreover, if a lady became now not married, she grow to be frequently left unfastened to live as she wanted, with out interference from simply all and sundry within the village.

The marriage agreement that was negotiated in advance than the nuptials were taken generally dictated how the own family's property had been to be divided up as soon because the divorce have come to be very last. They moreover had the proper to reclaim their dowries if a wedding ended — a proper women in one of a kind international locations throughout Europe did not very own.

Although the men were identified due to the fact the "ruler" inner their home, women most usually had a characteristic each bit as lively and authoritative as her husband. When their husbands have been absent, Norse ladies had full energy and authority over their household and circle of relatives industrial business enterprise. It changed right right into a function a lady would tackle without a doubt in the occasion her husband died.

As a photo of her essential feature as a manager of the family home and organization, many ladies in Viking Age Scandinavia have been buried with keys. Furthermore, no longer like women in modern-day European cultures, women in Scandinavia may moreover need to simply upward thrust quite high on the same time as accruing power, wealth, and status in their very personal – a truth borne out with the useful aid of the lavish burial mounds that contained ladies.

One instance of such became a girl idea to be a noble, or probably a queen, whose burial mound became determined in at Oseberg in Norway. She become buried in a lavishly carved deliver that become nearly seventy-one ft lengthy thru nearly seventeen feet huge and had a mast of thirty-3 or so. Although the grave have been disturbed and the valuable items have been taken, severa regular, extra mundane objects have been left in the back of. But how she was buried, similarly to any male noble, suggests that women may also want to maintain a place of excessive esteem in Scandinavian culture.

There is one famous myth that one sees accomplished out in well-known way of life over and over once more. Moreover, this is the parable of the defend maiden and the concept that women have been equal to guys within the state of affairs of battle. The History Channel show Vikings depicts Lagertha, spouse of Ragnar, as being a powerful warrior who often fights alongside the guys in struggle. Later on, after turning into a Jarl herself, Lagertha will growth an navy of protect maidens inclined to combat and die for her.

This isn't always to say that ladies did now not combat alongside men. They did. Archaeological evidence, similarly to fashionable-day debts, relate reminiscences of women preventing with the guys on the arena of warfare. One such account is the Siege of Dorostolon in Bulgaria in 971 CE. It become said that the victors have been greatly surprised to discover women a number of the useless.

Women fought, but it became no longer almost as excellent as famous subculture makes it out to be. So an extended manner because the historic report shows, there had been no prepared legions of informed guard maidens.

Women's place in Scandinavian society, at the equal time as perhaps no longer same to men, have turn out to be certainly head and shoulders above the station of ladies in present day European societies.

Chapter 6: Viking Religion

As the Scandinavians centralized their power and common international places collectively with Norway, Sweden, and Denmark, they transformed from their antique ideals – a pagan faith to Christianity towards the cease of the Viking Age. Some students trust it have come to be the aim of forming sturdy alliances with Christian international places like France and England. In evaluation, one-of-a-kind college students believe it turned into from being in such near proximity to Christian missionaries – both thru the taking of slaves or evangelical missions – that triggered the eventual conversion of the Scandinavian countries.

However, preceding to the conversion of the Scandinavians, they practiced a totally complicated faith complete of many gods, extraordinary geographical areas, frost giants, and a very last war that might give up the arena. The Vikings believed the give up of the world became predestined, and even though people may additionally want to conflict and fight closer to it, there was now not something that could be finished to change it.

Old Norse faith states that there are 9 particular geographical regions, they all associated with the resource of an sizeable ash tree called Yggdrasil. The 9 worlds are Asgard (realm of the Aesir), Alfheim (realm of the Bright Elves), Jotunheim (realm of the Giants), Midgard (realm of the humans), Muspell (realm of fireplace), Nidavellir (realm of the Dwarves), Niflheim (realm of ice and mist), Svartalfheim (realm of the Black Elves), and Vanaheim (realm of the Vanir).

The 9 nation-states all co-existed with every distinctive and will hold going for walks together till Ragnarok — the final warfare that could result in the end of the place.

Like many pagan religions, the Norse had been polytheistic, the high-quality in their gods become Odin, the Allfather of the Aesir. They worshipped Frigg, Freya, Thor, Loki, and Hel, amongst others. Like some of the gods from distinctive polytheistic religions, every of the gods modified into imbued with particular developments. Furthermore, like some of the gods from the vintage religions, they exhibited all too human dispositions at instances.

However, the Norse divided their gods into awesome corporations – the Aesir and the Vanir. Those groups engaged in a battle that spanned a long time, preventing most effective while every facets decided out they have been similarly matched. After that, they co-existed with one another.

In the Norse faith, it's far believed that on the equal time as folks that died a regular death – infection, age, and so forth. – traveled to at least one version of the underworld. Half of the soldiers who died in struggle, even though, traveled to Valhalla to dinner party with precise combatants and

Odin as they waited for Ragnarok. The different half of the fallen warriors traveled to Freya's hall, Folkvangr, to examine for the very last war.

On the day of Ragnarok, a ship known as Naglfar – fabricated from the fingernails and toenails of fallen warriors – will ferry those in Valhalla and Forkvangr to the fight.

Ragnarok is the final struggle an extremely good manner to no longer truly save you the area but will declare the lives of a number of the gods – Odin, Thor, Freya, and Loki. The global is probably submerged in water. Once that is accomplished, the arena will resurface, renewed, and fertile once more. The global might be repopulated via manner of people who can be welcomed by way of using the gods who live on Ragnarok.

That is the fast and dirty, oversimplified model of the vintage Norse faith. It is what we have been taught about the religion of the Vikings for day trip of mind. However, as with the whole lot else, it's far up for scholarly debate.

In his ebook, Myths of the Pagan North: The Gods of the Norsemen, Professor Christopher Abram argues the idea that notions of Valhalla, Ragnarok, and the Norse afterlife may not had been as widespread as humans trust. Abrams argues that the notion in Valhalla can also were a literary introduction written on the behest of the ruling elegance because of the fact the concept of useless warriors having to combat once more for a lord mirrors the social systems of the day. Abram is going on to quote the dearth of an archaeological report to buttress his argument about the dearth of full-size belief in Valhalla.

However, there may be an archaeological file that refutes Abram's argument. There have been numerous archaeological exhibits that very truely depict a notion in Valhalla and Ragnarok. Thorwald's Cross, located at the Isle of Man and dated as being constructed someplace the various tenth and 11th centuries, surely indicates what appears to be Odin being fed on by means of the use of way of Fenrir at Ragnarok. Later interpretations have made the argument that it's miles Jesus winning over Satan, and however, nowhere in Christian iconography is Jesus depicted with a raven or eagle on his shoulder, bolstering the argument that it's far a scene depicting Ragnarok as an opportunity.

The Gosforth Cross, located in Cumbria, England, dates lower returned to the middle of the tenth century. Although there are ornamental panels and what appears to be a Christian crucifixion, most of the carvings at the Gosforth Cross depict what very surely seems to be activities at Ragnarok.

Other archaeological finds, which consist of the Ledberg Stone and Skarpaker Stone, every in Sweden and relationship to for the duration of the eleventh century, further to special discoveries, are presupposed to depict various scenes from Ragnarok. It have to appear that with discoveries at unique elements and unique times within the worldwide, there may be, in reality, an archaeological record and suggests that a belief within the old Norse faith can also were more everyday than Abram appears to trust.

That belief within the vintage faith may additionally were filtered away and watered down over the years, with the Christianization of the Scandinavian international locations, however the vintage faith does seem to had been a effective strain for a long term the various Norse human beings.

Chapter 7: What Did The Vikings Play?

The Viking is largely an inhabitant of Scandinavia and a farmer - a person like every other at that aspect. It isn't always surprising that he additionally created his private lifestyle, which covered bodily and intellectual enjoyment. What did the Scandinavians play in the Middle Ages and how did it have an impact on their subculture?

In famous life-style, a function photo of a Scandinavian warrior suggests him as a depraved guy, brutal man, ,a killer - a barbarian. It is a very deceptive photo, even though identified with the nineteenth and twentieth century Vikings, which emerge as later reproduced through filmmakers or writers and because of this became rooted in the minds of modern people. Scandinavian way of existence from the early Middle Ages is described by the usage of an increasing number of latest courses of distant places and native researchers, showing the medieval inhabitant of Scandinavia as someone who isn't very unique from his peers from the relaxation of Europe. An thrilling prospect of assembly with this "actual Viking" might be to study his amusement. This hassle rely is handled in this text, because of the truth like simply anybody, additionally a "viking" had his video video games.

The deliver basis for getting to know about Scandinavian sports sports sports sports in the Middle Ages are Icelandic sagas - a massive series of testimonies approximately Icelanders, Scandinavian kings and legends of the North. Although they may be in huge part fictional, they incorporate essential information approximately current-day lifestyles. Sagas written because of the reality the surrender of the 12th century are divided via researchers into the subsequent instructions: sagas about Icelanders, royal sagas, mythical sagas, bishop's sagas, translated European romances. They comprise descriptions of sports for the cause that settlement of Iceland spherical 872, which frequently state of affairs normal existence. Although in the ninth century Icelanders did now not understand the writing, the content material fabric of the sagas end up exceeded on orally, from era to technology. Most sagas were no longer written until about 400 years later, in the thirteenth century.

Reading the sagas we are in a position to analyze plenty about sports sports sports activities sports in medieval Scandinavia. However, the reader encounters many problems in finding a super answer to the question "What and the way modified into it completed? Nowadays, if there may be for example a football fit in the e-book, does the author take the problem to present an explanation for the pointers of this group game? Even if a person isn't always inquisitive about soccer, they recognise extra or a terrific deal much much less the recommendations of football. It modified into comparable with sagamanders (writing sagas), who usually did not feel the want to provide an explanation for a given game, due to the truth with the useful resource of assumption, it become appeared to a much wider audience. How is this viable? Medieval Iceland changed into inhabited via using about 50,000 people, who met numerous instances a three hundred and sixty five days in a bigger or smaller group at rallies - this is how the information modified into carried.

From the whole body of belongings, several video video games may be positioned (there may be a temptation to use the phrase "pastime", but in our expertise of the phrase, it seemed simplest within the nineteenth century), which were incredibly well-known: glima, knattleikr, sund, hestaþin

Glima, due to the fact the most effective bodily hobby said, has the whole right to be known as a recreation. This is the call of Icelandic wrestling, which continues to be the national enterprise of Icelanders in recent times. There is even an worldwide glyma affiliation. This kind of undertaking has its equivalents in all cultures round the sector. The etymology of this phrase refers to "joy", "a laugh", "clarity". It is difficult to search for the origins of the glyma inside the springs, because of the reality this kind of natural rivalry have to have appeared lots earlier, even in historical instances. The Icelandic model defined in the sagas is extra brutal than the modern stock. In sagas we are capable to differentiate severa unique techniques, which might be virtually described with the aid of way of the use of sagamanders. It isn't always unusual for us to observe approximately throws of opposition that brought about immoderate accidents, mutilations or possibly dying of 1 in each of them. Often the game fans described in sagas have been slaves or "monsters" which shows that they had been particularly expert for such obligations. Most of the slaves came from Ireland, and that they were referred to as svartr, or "blacks". (because of the reality their complexions were darker than Icelandic ones). It is suggested that, like most of the competition, the glyma need to have "come" to Iceland from Ireland.

The next game to be placed within the lyrics is knattleikr, or "ball sport". Unfortunately, there are a number of unknowns proper right here Based at the property, a few facts may be supplied as follows: This is a group game, for which sticks and balls were used, the pitch end up in a manner marked and achieved mostly on the frozen floor of the lake or fjord. And that is it. Unfortunately, we are not capable of find out what have been the rules of this sport, or what number of players the crew come to be crafted from. Some researchers compare it to lacrosse, grass hockey or baseball. However, none of those sports sports sports may be a right away inheritor to the guidelines of knattleikr, due to the fact they were created heaps later and in Europe many video video games within the Middle Ages used the ball. This activity required super agility and, due to the fact the sagamanders write, have become now not for everyone. Young boys and men executed one by one. In flip, ladies can also additionally want to best watch the video games. People who had been too aggressive or had issues with power of will had been moreover excluded. This was for safety motives - the fits regularly led to a brawl. Very frequently we are capable of locate such descriptions of video games in sagas, all through which gamers use glimmer strategies to knock down the opponent. Sometimes they gain for sticks that harm on each distinctive.

The ball recreation can be decided within the Middle Ages every in France and in the British Isles, from wherein it in all likelihood reached Iceland, wherein the guidelines were tailored to their very very personal alternatives.

Sund, or swimming, have become furthermore well-known. However, the decision is wrong, because it had little to do with modern-day pastime swimming (fantastic, there were such competitions, however obviously they bored the Scandinavians). Swimming defined within the sagas isn't always some thing but wrestling in water! It consisted in mutual melting of the fighters till any of them might have had enough, or at the same time as the spectators, being the referees, decided to win taken into consideration considered one of them.

The remaining form of leisure can be the most interesting - hestaþing is otherwise "horse stopping". Icelanders concealed specific horses for fights, which fee more than mares or gelding. Often competitions have been organized in which many competitors took element, a sort of championship, e.G. Between one element of a fjord and the alternative. Horses could fight with each specific via kicking and biting, and the simplest who allow move, might lose. The horse represented its owner, and all the splendor fell on him after winning the fight. Although this entertainment may additionally seem very peculiar and brutal, it is even extra surprising that it is nevertheless practiced in some international places of Southeast Asia (sic!). There also are a few warning symptoms and signs about dogfights, however there's most effective one saga that announces it without delay.

Apart from widely defined types of bodily hobby, sagas moreover encompass pores and skin throwing, pores and skin or rope dragging (skinnleikur, stangarstökk), archery (skotbakki, bogfimi), long and sprint racing (langhlaup, spretthlaup), horse racing (burtreiðar, atreið), stone or spear throwing (steinakast, spjótkast), gymnastics (fimleikar) and numerous strength assessments (aflraunir). In a way we also can talk about opposition in ingesting or consuming!

Surprisingly, in sagas we won't enjoy any pastime connected with snowboarding or skating, which may be only used for movement (perhaps there was no need to install writing down approximately it?), notwithstanding the truth that there was a god Ullr who used skis.

Games and bodily interest were the concept of Scandinavian life-style. Through competitions organized most of the whole island's community (e.G. The Icelandic championships, which may be confirmed inside the assets), on the best hand, conflicts had been avoided, and however, the possibility became created to ventilate younger prodigality and permit for body schooling. Thanks to the victories in competitions of the location or the whole island, the Icelander received recognition and turn out to be later called the maximum effective of the island's population inside the sagas that favoured his family. The representatives of the location felt answerable for him and their "fans" created a sense of brotherly love and neighborhood identification. Additionally, they contributed to the physical improvement of the younger guys and skilled them as warriors.

Physical professions had been furthermore a part of severa customs and traditions (also created) which include rallies (þingi), non secular holidays (disablót), celebrations of ordinary existence - funeral, birthday, birthday, annual vacations - equinoxes, solstices, Sundays (in the submit-Christianization technology). The places in which the video video games had been first of all held have been converted with the useful resource of the use of the game fanatics and the culture from a panorama into a very precise vicinity - a place of play seemed in some unspecified time inside the destiny of the island. Later on, community names were created that noted video games or a particular game along with hestaþingshóll in Iceland. Finally, they have been a law-making detail (the oldest Icelandic series of laws mentions horse combating and the consequences of bad practices) and had been also a transmitter of worship from one cultural circle to every other (e.G. From the British Isles to Iceland).

Chapter 8: Female Characters In The Viking Global

Vikings are commonly related to the cruel male global of wars, and the not unusual guy, whilst asked about their religion, will first factor out Thor and Lokie, identified from Marvel films, and from time to time can even factor out Walhalla. However, female characters additionally play a number one role in myths and sagas. They are dad or mum spirits in addition to partners of warriors. They are often no a good deal less valiant than they are. We realise them in particular from mentions within the sagas and Edda poetic.

One of the maximum essential dad or mum spirits have been dis, goddesses related to fertility and lack of existence. The earliest factor out of them is contained in the First Merserburgical Spell . In the poetry of the scalds, the phrase disa changed into a synonym of a girl, given to each noble-born lady .

According to Jan de Vries, the word disa derives from dha, i.E. To gift, and technique a being who gives mom's milk and care . The cult of dis confirms the toponomy of all Scandinavia. Their night meal modified into celebrated in mid-October. The dis had been asked to help at some point of childbirth, at the same time as inside the rest of a person's existence they seemed as his or her guardians. They were associated not best with people, however furthermore with complete families. In sagas they frequently appear as spadisir, or prophetic dis, and promise to assist the hero in war, on occasion defensive him from the hail of arrows and spears (e.G. Inside the Wolsung circle of relatives's saga, in which they cope with Siegfried). Like fights, they may be associated with stopping and conflict. At that point they had been referred to as imun-disir, i.E. Disy stopping. It have emerge as moreover on occasion that, appearing in a dream, they anticipated someone's death.

Similar to them (most probable the same) have been the fylgias, defined in sagas as supernatural, being concerned spirits taking the shape of ladies or animals. The word phylogy in Irish technique the membrane or placenta. Sometimes the same shape of superhuman babysitter become referred to as a disa in poetry, and in prose a phylogy, therefore their in all likelihood identification. Beings with comparable tendencies were moreover referred to as hamingja or horse, or female.

In the animal shape, the phylogy had adjust ego tendencies. Similarly to the dis, the phylogies looked after not best people, however moreover whole families. They did now not continuously appear for my part, they often seemed in companies. The most often one want to look their fylgias of their sleep. Only a loss of life or destined loss of life character have end up capable of see it in easy sight, and this intended that the groove turned into parted with him.

To sum up: disks and silhouettes belonged to at the least one beauty of supernatural girl characters looking after a person at start, all through his lifetime, and then leading him into the afterlife. They were intended to provide advice to the characters and warn them approximately the hazard.

After their death, the infantrymen have been sorted by using way of the use of various supernatural beings - the battleships, which selected the bravest to deliver them to Walhalla. Their call comes from the noun val, or fallen, and the verb kjosa - to pick out. They can consequently be interpreted as those who took warriors from the battlefield or chose which of the residing to die in war. Often the warring parties fell in love with the infantrymen and feature grow to be their earthly companions. In Eddie Poetry, they appear as supernatural guardians of the heroes, then as their companions condemned to the often tragic destiny of earthly girls.

Broomhilda, loved Sigurda, is an example. She is first referred to within the Song of Sygrdif, of which she is the principle character. As a battle, she showed disobedience to Odin, giving victory to a warrior to whom Alfödr had destined dying. "Odin, in revenge for this, punished her with the thorn of sleep. He sentenced her to by no means win the war another time and she or he or he have to need to marry" . Nine But she swore that she may want to now not marry a person who changed into afraid. She fell asleep in a defend city, surrounded via way of manner of a mystical flame, simply so no coward ought to get into it. Only the courageous Siegfried woke her up. Valkyrie taught him magical runes and informed him many secrets and techniques and strategies and strategies. Then he took her as his partner.

According to certainly one of a type debts, Sigurd met Brunhild at the court docket of Heimar, her brother-in-law and protector.

He observed her even as, seeking out his falcon, he climbed the tower in which she spent her time, stitching on the fabric with the golden thread of his conflict. He fell in love together along with her and desired to marry her, but she stubbornly refused, claiming that her destiny, as a Valerian, become warfare, at the same time as he modified into to marry Gudrun, the daughter of King Gjuki. But while he did not provide in, she agreed.

An excerpt from Song of the Song of the Siegfried and the Saga of Wölsung tells the tale of processes in some time Siegfried, deluded in spells, forgot approximately Brunhild and tricked into assisting Gunnar, his buddy, to get her for his partner. When she decided out about this, she fell into anger and made her married Gunnar take revenge. "I offer you with a preference," she stated to him. - Or thou shalt do now not anything, after which I will go away thee and pass lower lower back to my house, and thou shalt lose wealth and power Or thou shalt kill Sigurd. And his son, lest [] he ever take revenge for his father's loss of lifestyles". Gunnar fulfilled her request and sent the youngest of the brothers, Gottarma, who did no longer input into blood brotherhood with Sigurd, to kill him. After this crime, Brunhilda alas devoted suicide.

Walkies had been often involved within the initiation of the protagonist, as verified in Song of Helga. The call character is a extra youthful guy without a name and speech talents. Once, sitting on a mound, he located 9 waltzes dashing on horses. One of them, Swawawa, spoke to him, and the formerly silent Helga spoke for the primary time. The preventing gave him a call, confirmed him in which to locate the top notch sword, after which shielded him in conflict. She have emerge as his companion, however it's miles emphasised that she become although a combating female. Soon after, Helgi fell in war, but the music ends with the assertion that "Helgi and Swawa have been reborn yet again.

Another of the songs speaks in their incarnations - Helgim of the Ylfing family and the Sygrun martial arts. At her request, Helgi fought King Hödbrodd, whom she did no longer need to marry, and he obtained, however his father and one of the Sygrun brothers additionally died in warfare. Valkyrie have become Helga's partner, but rapid afterwards he have become murdered via using the use of a vengeful, surviving brother of Sygrun. Odin allowed Helga to meet his spouse for a few more nights after his death, however she rapid died of grief and longing. At the stop of this music it additionally seems that Sygrun and Helga had been to be born once more, he as Helga Haddingjaskati and she or he as Kora Halfdanardottir. And in step with the Song of the Bark have grow to be a war.

The motif of flax spinning or weaving is also associated with the waltzes, that is associated with their photograph of the spinning of future. In the Soot of Nyal, with the aid of weaving a magic cloth, they've got an impact on the direction of the Battle of Clontarf, fought in Ireland in 1014. In this piece we study: "On Good Friday it befell in Katanes [northern Scotland] that a person named Dorrudr got here out (from home). He observed twelve horsemen arrive on the house of the work of the unknowns (dyngja); everybody disappeared there. And he regarded out the window and observed that there have been girls weaving on looms within the room. Human heads served as weights, and in location of warp and weft they woven human intestines, a sword modified into for the water, and an arrow for the fence.

The commonplace feature of the characters said above is each their dating to human destiny and the truth that they will be female deities who bestow upon guy. Disy and fylgie seem with the man or woman on the day of his beginning and accompany him through existence, supporting and looking after him. The Walkies, as an alternative, cover the warrior in battle and ensure that he leaves this worldwide at the appointed time, once in a while additionally they end up his earthly partners. They are ready to do an awful lot within the name of affection, but even as betrayed, they may be capable of take merciless revenge, as may be anticipated from Viking women.

To be girls inside the Viking global

It is broadly believed that early medieval Scandinavia become ruled through way of manner of the Vikings. However, Icelandic sagas inform us approximately a warrior known as Freydhis, who in one of the skirmishes embarrassed an entire Viking unit. It seems that this kind of immoderate social characteristic of a Viking girl turn out to be not anything precise...

Men, regardless of their domination, did no longer have specific electricity in Scandinavia. There are many legends approximately volatile and effective ladies, who very often aroused fear among their companions. One such girl changed into the well-known Deep Thinking Aud, who (fast after her husband's dying) sailed to Iceland and took ownership of the complete valley of the Hvammu Fjord. Moreover, it's also recognized that spherical 900 years in the past it changed into the maximum crucial agreement in Iceland. Commonly considered to be "deeply wealthy", it took possession of huge regions of land, dividing them among character participants of household and servants.

Another instance of a very rich Scandinavian female (said in the departments via Thietmar and Adam Bremenski) have come to be Świętosława, additionally referred to as Sigida Storrad or Gunhilda. She was the daughter of Mieszko I. Additionally, spherical 980 or 984 she married Eryk Zwycięski, king of Sweden. Many medievalists agree with that it have become a political marriage, concluded in competition to Denmark. It modified into purported to allow Mieszko to reinforce his Piast strength in Western Pomerania. The most effective toddler from this dating come to be Olaf, later king of Sweden. Around 995 the queen have emerge as widowed, however, essential to the formation of a Swedish-Danish alliance towards Norway. She sealed this alliance together at the side of her subsequent marriage to Swen Forkbeard, king of Sweden and Denmark. Five youngsters had been born from Sigrida's second marriage, of whom have turn out to be the following kings of Sweden. It is nicely well well worth citing at this element that Svatoslava have become also the mom of the Great Canon, one of the legendary rulers of early medieval Europe.

It is also very vital to realise that a person may additionally want to have become a complete-fledged ruler (even from the royal circle of relatives) satisfactory on the corner. In addition, there are signs that girls can also inherit the land from their mother and father, and there was a possibility to inherit a part of the land for a male descendant. In archaeological belongings it's miles very seen amongst burials, the most famous of it's the boat tomb from Oseberg. Usually women were buried with very wealthy fixtures, which they may suit with guys. The items have been very prestigious, but had a awesome person than those determined in guys's graves. They have been regularly sewing utensils, kitchen devices and stylish jewelry.

The role of the girls of Vikings have come to be very crucial at a few degree in the summer time. When men went to wars, it turn out to be the women who had to take care of the family and the soil. Many of these girls later have come to be widows who had relationships with their brother or someone who came from the proper now circle of relatives of their late husband. Very often in Scandinavia there have been additionally polygamous widow unions, which were legally familiar.

The Scandinavian lady changed into capable of discover herself very well in a global dominated through the use of courageous Vikings. She completed a notably critical role in society, and crook provisions and Scandinavian lifestyle allowed her to recognize her very very own plans and goals. In addition, she changed into the caretaker of the house campfire, and needed to cope with the cultivation of the land.

Chapter 9: A Atypical Viking Ritual

The Vikings are considered to be one of the bloodiest professions ever to exist. This is said of them because of their strength and ruthlessness at some level inside the invasions.

The bloody eagle is an interesting ritual and virtually debatable. Its symbolism and specificity had been the difficulty of dialogue to in the meanwhile. According to vintage files, it become in truth imagined to exist and to arouse horror among folks who understand the manner it goes. Many researchers also declare that it is the pleasant argument confirming statistics approximately the ruthlessness and cruelty of Vikings.

The first model of the ritual worries pulling out lungs. First the convict changed into immobilized face down. The subsequent diploma changed into to interrupt out and bend the ribs in this sort of way as to shape wings. Then the injuries were sprinkled with salt. The closing element become the tearing out of the lungs, which have been spread at the ribs. The body massacred in this way fashioned some element much like the wings on which the killed person became to fly to Odin. There is likewise speak of every special model of this punishment, which may be very similar. Instead of lungs, the Vikings might tear out the blades, which may additionally additionally provide the sufferer's frame the shape of wings.

There are many rituals that relate to giving such items to the gods. Odin is a creature who along with his conduct and look fits perfectly into the advent of the Vikings. According to mythology he's ruthless, bloodthirsty, terrible and unpredictable. The offers made to Odin with the resource of the Vikings were merciless, fancy and truly bloody.

Scientists are however arguing about whether or no longer or no longer this ritual definitely existed. Interestingly, everyday with many money owed, best the eagle grow to be drawn on its once more so that you should see the ribs, which does no longer display that they had been damaged. It is also viable that this is nice a literary fiction, which end up to expose the Vikings as a brutal kingdom and to warn in opposition to their invasions. Among the diverse messages there are a few inconsistencies which show that the ritual of the bloody eagle is unfathomable.

4 Shamans and Vikings

Traces of primitive beliefs which consist of animism, shamanism and totemism are in recent times an increasingly more famous state of affairs of research thru historians coping with the religiousness of pagan Indo-European peoples. This research isn't confined to educational speak, however additionally has an effect on shaping the picture of the depraved (e.G. The openly effeminate determine of "God's Madman"

Flocky in Michael Hirst's collection) or on agencies reconstructing vintage beliefs.

A specially thrilling relic of historic beliefs is the presence inside the religiousness of Scandinavians the stays of shamanism. The studies community does no longer simply agree at the query whether or not or now not or not shamanism constitutes a separate non secular gadget, or whether or not it's miles great a complementary detail to distinct religious systems. Elements of the shamanic belief tool have intermingled with all religions. Shamanism is occasionally the massive pillar of the beliefs of a given network (e.G. Within the beliefs of Siberian peoples), at the equal time as at other times it plays a aspect feature near the primary currents of religiousness (as within the Scandinavians), and however over again it performs a minor or even persecuted function in monotheistic religions (as maximum of the Muslim Turkish Alawites, i.E. The Alevi and Bectasiites, or in some Pentecostal beliefs amongst Christians).

The essential parent of shamanism is the shaman. His role is based totally on setting up touch with that worldwide. He can do so a splendid manner to carry out e.G. The function of a healer or a psychopomposed. A shaman has the strength of touch and vision of the opportunity international, however that lets in you to apply this strength to the entire, he occasionally has to gain for specific way, amongst which there are practices which include prayer, setting up verbal exchange through symbols or images. However, the maximum critical, key mission that constitutes the essence of shamanism is to set up direct contact. The shaman establishes it via introducing himself into an ecstatic kingdom. Until nowadays, fashions of falling into ecstasy have been remarkable - flight to distinct worlds (heaven or hell) or incarnation of spirits in oneself (such incarnation isn't always similar to possession in that the shaman, in region of the possessed one, controls his state). However, extra present day research has verified that there are cultures wherein the version of tour to the world of spirits does not exist (e.G. In Korea), and studies on publish-sessional cults and the so-known as shamanic ailment has demonstrated that a newbie adept of shamanic practices does not must have manipulate over his state. A shaman candidate, as a manner to be able to go to the afterlife and perform his function, should go through an initiation containing the myth of loss of life and rebirth.

The shaman is accompanied with the useful resource of way of his worrying or assisting spirit. This spirit is, in a manner, the shaman's 2nd ego, his double, shadow or perhaps filling. This being most often takes at the shape of an animal, but the demanding spirit additionally may be a plant or perhaps every other character. The maximum common symbolic, even symbolic animal-spirit of care is a chook of prey. Such a disturbing entity, which accompanies shamans in their rituals and is a part of the myths of the peoples residing on the Baltic Sea, modified into a predatory chook - a raven in Scandinavia, a horn in the Slavs or a falcon or an eagle inside the Baltic Sea.

There are 3 types of contact that a shaman establishes with a ghost:

complete identification - the shaman behaves definitely according with the need of the spirit who enters the shaman's frame and takes manipulate over it;

doubling the placement - the shaman performs every his very private and the spirit's feature; the form of this dating takes the form of a talk wherein the shaman talks to the spirit;

Verbal Reproduction - the shaman, via an define, presents the spirit he sees and, for example, remarks at the activities he sees, or tales visions that he summarizes after returning to a ordinary nation of recognition.

Another detail nicely worth citing is the fact that the deceased is followed on his way to that worldwide with the beneficial useful resource of zoomorphic beings - a falcon and a mount. Both in the whole Eurasian place and beyond, diverse parent ghosts appeared inside the shape of a chook. E.G. In many prairie Indian cultures there can be the Bird of Thunder, and the Black Bird appears in Turkish peoples, a raven or an eagle - in Yakuts, and in Indo-European peoples there are Garuda, the Persian Simurg or the Slavic Horn9. Also inside the Scandinavians, holy birds of prey or scavenging birds accompanied the splendid shaman king, Odin (already in the twelfth century Snoria Sturlosson decided that Odin have to have been a super leader, a king-priest and modified into venerated as a god). Odin's companions are ravens - Hugin

(Thought) and Munin (Memory), which each day bring him statistics approximately what is taking location in nine worlds. In the Prussians, those chook parent spirits accompany the deceased on his way to that worldwide. This is evidenced with the useful resource of the outline of the burial contained within the Dean's treatise, wherein the Teutonic Knights Tulisses and Ligaschs, defined with the aid of manner of the Teutonic Knights due to the fact the clergymen, record the deceased going to heaven within the company of a falcon and a horse.

Another characteristic of shamanism and happening within the Viking international is a particular kind of erotic family people. One of the non-public belongings of spiritual experience in historical times changed into the presentation of the sexual act as a mysterious and transcendental experience. The intimate dating current in shamanism some of the father or mother spirit and the shaman is an instance of this.

In the case of a shaman's whole identity with the spirit, the stressful spirit, that is generally of the other sex (as within the Scandinavian Female Fylgia) than the shaman, is in a way complementary to the priest-shaman being. Such a dating often consequences inside the phenomenon of sexual transgression. In some peoples, e.G. North American Indians, a few shamans are obliged to wear ladies's garb, and in Chukczów there are gay shamans who have to formalize the connection with the spirit in addition to the earthly partner.' Herodot, instead, mentions a tribe living in "Scythia, whose men bleed like girls every month. A similar situation is observed in Scandinavians - in Scandinavian myths the determine of Seidcony appears. It is normally defined as a sorceress or sorceress, i.E. A character who practises the seidr magic taught with the aid of the goddess Freya of the Wan own family. It lets in humans to advantage supernatural capabilities, that could each harm enemies and assist e.G. In the Wolsungi Saga, it lets in to alternate the form of people or make quick journeys. Volva (the bard), however, who wielded the magic of the seidr, come to be capable of bury the future and knew all of the secrets and techniques and strategies. This magic became practiced specifically with the resource of girls, in spite of the reality that men and women did not shrink back from it, although it come to be related to the disgrace of homosexuality. Such a scenario happened inside the case of Odin and Lokie, while the previous accused the latter of each homosexuality and hermaphroditism (which changed proper into a purpose to banish, and someone unjustifiably accused of such acts can also moreover need to kill the slanderer inside the Scandinavian international without any outcomes). However, Loki himself replied to Odin's charge.

Veiztu, ef ek gaf þeim er ek gefa né skylda,inum slævurom, sigr,átta vetrvartu fyr jörð neðankýr mólkandi properly enough kona,adequate hefr þú þar börn borit,

exact sufficient hugða ek þat args aðalEn þik síða kóðu Sámseyu í,right enough draptu á vétt sem völur,vitka líki fórtu verþjóð yfir,excellent sufficient hugða ek þat args aðal

Loki uses the term völur, it really is a bard (plural of Volvo), which indicates that Odin himself plays magic characteristic of girls. Furthermore, he calls Odin a peasant harlot, or args aðal (genuinely a woman manner). The courting among gay and divorced practices right to the fiddlers seems inseparable. Neither Odin nor Loki deny that they may be worried in lady ritual practices. Seidr and Galdr) have been the most not unusual shape of magic inside the Scandinavian global. Traces of the usage of seidr may be found in Scandinavia, Iceland, and in an area in which the Viking international intertwined with the arena of Sam.

The burials of fellows practicing seidr contained elements characteristic for girls, consisting of phallic wooden wands or a cauldron. Persons jogging towards such magic were buried as they lived, at the outskirts of the settlements far from the relaxation of the network but with appreciate due to the powerful.

Today, research on the role of sexual and shamanistic practices has a top effect on the improvement of neopagan moves. Some neo-pagan agencies, which incorporates the British fans of Ásatrú, don't forget homosexual practices to be unmanly and anti-circle of relatives - sincerely ignoring the artwork of scientists reading the phenomenon of ritual homosexuality some of the Scandinavians. Other neo-pagan corporations advocated with the aid of the Wiccan movement (despite the fact that Wicca's founder Gerald Gardner himself changed into quite "homosceptical") frequently emphasize the girl side of nature and emphasize that during spite of the reality that a heterosexual man can exercising seidr, homosexuals are more likely to obtain this. It remains an open query as to how a bargain impact seidr practices have had on the every day lives of Scandinavians and what kind of affect in addition research can also have on neo-pagan actions.

Chapter 10: Thirteen Days Of Plundering Lisbon

They fell on the shorelines of current day Spain like a cloud of locusts. To locations that have not said struggle for generations, they carried fireside and destruction. What booty did they manage to capture, what places to raze to the ground? And did the Vikings' raids on Andalusia go away an enduring mark on this wealthy land?

The emperors of [Andalusia] needed to battle no longer extraordinary with rebellious governors and French troops. The troubles may additionally additionally want to have come inside the least expected shape. In the middle of the ninth century Seville, the second one biggest metropolis of Al-Andalus, has cherished peace for a hundred and fifty years.

The emperors of Córdoba, 100 and fifty kilometers away, quite tons suppressed the rise up of the Yemenite Arabs, who rebelled in the seventies. Abd ar-Rahman II has just finished the improvement of a giant mosque in Seville, and the metropolis, situated within the midst of fertile fields and groves, has experienced a lush increase.

It became an outlet for the whole place, rich in olives, figs, grain and cattle, and had a looking for and selling port which Guadalquivir, the "huge river", associated with the capital city in the east and the Atlantic Ocean in the west. However, this useful area have become the purpose of its perdition whilst, in October 844, fifty-four boats with their beaks topped with dragon heads nailed to the grassy financial group of the river.

Hundreds of grown, bearded Scandinavians jumped out of them and, with battle shouts, rolling out their axes, fell into the unspoiled metropolis. Vikings got here to Al-Andalus. The population were in panic. After the theft of Seville, the Scandinavian invaders loaded the loot and captured inhabitants on the drakkars and carried them lower lower back to the marshy labyrinth of the Guadalquivir Delta, where they set up camp.

They rapid received reinforcements and then decrease once more to Seville, which they plundered for every week, while Abd ar-Rahman despatched decided calls to the governors inside the south and collected forces to repel the invaders.

The arrival of the Vikings come to be no longer without a doubt unexpected, as within the preceding months a fleet of prolonged boats were circulating inside the Gulf of Bi-Skay and repulsed in Gijón and A Coruñi with the aid of the usage of Ramira I of Asturias. They had been luckier in Muslim Lisbon (Al-Ushbuna), which they plundered for thirteen days earlier than they sailed directly to Cadiz. From there, they went inland, looting with impunity the entirety that fell into their hands at the way. When Sevilla have become on hearth and its garrison modified into limping inside the fortresses, the metropolis's populace determined safe haven in close by Carmon (Karmuna), while the emir persevered to build up an military.

Then the significance of the magnates' borderline variables have end up very clear. Among individuals who added the troops became Musa Ibn Musa himself from Banu Kasi. The Viking invasion reconciled the Emir with the rebellious keep close of the borderland. Musa formally confirmed that he's a bona fide purchaser, for that reason gaining the Emir's approval as the ruler of the Upper March. Abd ar-Rahman, however, strengthened his function as a sovereign and used the army power of Banu Kasi.

As a cease quit end result, on November 11th, 844, the Vikings attacked from an ambush via the use of way of the Umayyajdzka pressure had been pushed out, and their boats were attacked with the aid of manner of "Greek fireplace", a napalm-like substance fired from throwers located on ships. They suffered heavy losses, and even as Abd ar-Rahman ordered to kill the captives at the battlefield, the survivors withdrew in panic.

After a chain of unsuccessful raids at the south coast and likely North Africa, the Vikings took the direction in their lands. For the Emir, the Battle of Seville became a triumph, so he despatched his heroes all the manner to the Maghreb to trumpet about his Victoria. About fourteen years later, the Vikings lower back. This time the emirate changed into prepared. In 858 the Muslim fleet crossed the Vikings' road off the Portuguese coast and their plan to ravage Guadalquivir's valley burned to the ground when they located out that Emir Muhammad I had sent the military to meet them.

The Scandinavians, who have been continuously in movement, averted a warfare together along along with his fleet and sailed eastwards through the Strait of Gibraltar. They captured Algeciras, burned down a mosque there (the number one one in Al-Andalus), and set up their base within the harbor. From there they sailed to the Maghreb, landed close to Nakuru, the capital of an independent Muslim us of a, which they plundered and from in which they took prisoners, collectively with girls from the ruling family.

Meanwhile, the Muslim fleet modified into directed at them once more, in order that they moved in addition east along the Andalusian coast. They attacked the Frankish Septimania and in the end set up a wintry weather camp within the marshy and uninhabited Camargue delta at the mouth of the Rhone.

In Mediterranean nations, as anywhere else, the success of the Vikings depended carefully at the element of marvel, specially when they invaded regions in which that that they'd now not needed to cope with threats from the sea for generations, consisting of the Al-Andalus coast.

The Scandinavians have surely moreover are to be had in for business functions, or as a minimum to promote or trade for jewels or some aspect they wanted, heaps a great deal less transportable loot and treasured community marketable prey, collectively with vital captives.

The captured human beings had been pressured to feature courses and lead them to their next places. After their reports in the English and French lands, they will communicate a touch Latin or take the clergy captured within the North as interpreters. Indeed, assets say that the Umayyads managed to shop for out girls from the ruling Nakur family, so some form of negotiation needed to take area.

Although for Muslim chroniclers the Vikings have been barbarians, or Madjus as they have been known as, Scandinavian subculture identifies their leaders as Björn Ironfoot and Hastein, sons of legendary Ragnar Lodbrok.

When wintry weather 859 ended, they sailed over again to Al-Andalus, but along the manner they attacked the Balearic Islands, where their fleet of Muhammad I attacked them. They couldn't danger any more losses, genuinely so they decided to move returned together and, with their ingenuity, outwitted the Muslims chasing them, headed inland.

The large and moderate Ebro come to be a waterway of precisely the kind that their boats were designed for. They sailed to Tortosa, wherein they grabbed their oars and sailed upstream at whole pace, leaving the Umayyads' fleet within the back of, depending on the wind. Outside the waterfalls near Flix, wherein they had to circulate their boats, they had an smooth adventure via the lands of Ban Kasi.

They sailed under the Roman bridge in Zaragoza and reached the Basque america of america of the usa. There they went ashore and rushed the captives with their loot earlier than them, fell on Pamplona and captured her King Garsey (son of Enek Aritza), for whose launch they demanded an exceptionally excessive ransom in coins.

And simply so they controlled to obtain the Bay of Biscay, recreate the fleet and sail domestic with the captives and the loot. The complete excursion lasted simply over a twelve months.

Although the Vikings' raids on Islamic Spain seduced the imagination of Muslim and Christian chroniclers, they did not cause longer contacts and had little lasting effect. It is stated that a number of the captured Scandinavians were given their lives and settled near Seville, wherein they have become cheesemakers (!), but that is due to a misreading of the Arabic chronicle.

Another deliver notes a diplomatic assignment despatched to Scandinavia underneath the manage of one of the favored al-Hakam poets, Jahji Ibn al-Hakam al-Ghazal, but it is also high-quality a legend. Nor have the Scandinavians advanced lasting exchange contributors of the family with Al-Andalus, as they did with the Abkhazian East. They can also need to satisfactory provide slaves, but at the equal time as there was superb call for for them, there was moreover a large supply within the form of prisoners taken within the route of the invasions to the Christian North or Gentiles captured in Eastern Europe and brought from there with the resource of French and Jewish consumers.

The nice myths approximately Vikings

A slight-haired, blue-eyed muscle guy who, collectively along with his companions in animal skins and feature helmets, regularly loot settlements at the coasts of England and France, raping and murdering whomever he falls for - that may be a image of a wicker seemed from films or novels. But is there a grain of fact in it?

I do not assume there are any warriors in European information about whom such a number of myths and legends had been written as approximately the Vikings. It seems, but, that the stereotypical attributes attributed to them do no longer continuously reflect the fact 100%. Not to mention the truth that a number of them are truely unfaithful! Here are 5 famous claims about brave Nordic warriors, which can be whole nonsense - or as a minimum a big abuse.

1. They had been robbers and looters who simplest had a conflict of their heads

The well-known Lindisfarne stone captures the wild, brutal invaders from the North who ransacked St. Kutbert's Church off the British coast in 793. As we examine in Robert Ferguson's ebook Hammer and Cross. The new Viking story, the bas-remedy "indicates seven marching men in profile. The figures on the front and back of the column are unarmed, likely due to the lack of region on the semicircular stone. Two center figures keep axes and 3 at the back of them swords. [] They march with their heads raised immoderate and torsoed, elevating their guns with one hand, as even though for the challenge of blow.

This and other ancient sources present the Vikings in a absolutely terrible slight. No wonder, consequently, that the image of Scandinavian peoples conveyed on the idea of this sort of "documentation" is as an opportunity gloomy. But does the black legend of Nordic warriors have a few factor to do with truth?

Well, at the least there may be a grain of reality in it. Some of the Vikings' expeditions have been clearly aggressive, but simply as often the medieval Scandinavians went out to sea to discover buying and promoting companions, searching out new places to settle or clearly out of herbal interest. And no matter the reality that they set out to loot, they had been generally guided with the beneficial aid of economic worries - not an innate propensity for violence.

The sight of the boat have become supposed to arouse fear many of the English and the French. However, there can be lots to suggest that the friends were usually happy to go to. They have been saying trade. The sight of the boat come to be alleged to arouse worry a number of the Englishmen and the French. However, there may be lots to signify that the friends had been at the entire glad to peer the boat. They had been saying exchange.

The raids at the British Isles and European coasts on the give up of the eighth century had been likely one of the many episodes because of Hunger. That is why they were not likely to appear during periods of prosperity - at that factor the populace of the North maintained proper contacts with their neighbours. The sagas handed down from technology to technology communicate as an lousy lot approximately wars as they do approximately touring to discover new lands.

Many Vikings, with the useful resource of the way, deserted wandering around to settle sincerely in one vicinity. This became the case, as an example, in Normandy, in which after stormy war escapades, with the anointing of Charles III Prostak, he settled down and became the Count of Rollon. This is how Bernard Cornwell describes the dichotomous nature of medieval Scandinavians in his bestselling novel The Last Kingdom:

They have been referred to as the Vikings after they had been dandelions coming to the ocean, and the Danes or pagans once they traded. The human beings of the 3 ships had been consequently taken into consideration Vikings because of the truth they burned and pillaged homesteads (). In each bay, port and estuary of every river they trembled for worry that prolonged Viking boats may suddenly emerge at the horizon. The dragons on their beaks have been terrified, the men crusing with these dragons have been afraid and prayed that God could spare them the fury of the Northerners.

2. They had blond hair, blue eyes and superhuman power

When we reflect onconsideration on wikings, we see a photo of slight-haired and blue-eyed guys, noticeably sturdy, brave and naturally competitive. The reality is, but, that those guys have been not extensively first rate from the standard inhabitant of Europe--they were slightly taller and of a barely heavier stature. So in which did the vision of sailing warriors come from?

After the famous attack at the monastery in Lindisfarne, this is the textual content: "That equal 12 months there had been horrible signs and symptoms and signs and symptoms over Northumbria, and that they terrified the human beings of Northumbria: uncommon lightning bolts have been lit and fiery dragons were seen flying in the air. Soon after these signs and symptoms and symptoms came a wonderful famine, and soon afterwards, the same year, pagan dandelions, like devils, pitifully destroyed the church of God in Lindisfarne, with rape and slaughter. The Catholic clergy feared the Vikings most of all. It is once in a while sudden: monasteries and church homes have been an smooth goal for dandruffers who did no longer comprehend the European idea of holiness. And it have become in massive factor clergymen and clergymen who have been responsible for the black PR throughout the Nordic warriors. They had been the first to present the "barbarians from the North" devilish tendencies.

The discovery of a barrow in 1880, in which the boat and the remains of a wicker have been buried, delivered oil to the fireplace.

As it grow to be confirmed with the useful resource of studies (completed best in 2007), it have become a body of a person spherical 40 years vintage, 181 cm tall - i.E. 15 cm above the common at that time - and with very heavy bones. It have to had been years earlier than it came to mild that the deceased suffered from an adenoma or pituitary tumour, which brought about him to show symptoms of giantism.

Meanwhile, within the nineteenth century, while the grave have turn out to be determined, scientists fast mixed statistics with ancient payments. The result have become a picture of a vicinage-olbaby. And it persists to in the interim, no matter the fact that modern, complete DNA exams completed with the useful resource of anthropologists display that people from the North - even though slightly taller than the not unusual - have been no longer so superior to the Englishmen or French whom they attacked (men measured 171 cm on commonplace and women - 158 cm).

What approximately hair colour? Well, scientists have now not placed any hints in this. It's feasible that blonde hair modified into the dominant coloration maximum of the Vikings of Swedish origin, but already Norwegians or Danes had as an opportunity darkish or crimson hair.

three. They wore helmets with horns

It's possibly the maximum famous fantasy approximately the Vikings - and yet the least correct. Horned headgear is frequently discovered at the pages of novels and films, at the identical time as archaeologists have not discovered any lines of such "fashion" amongst Scandinavians. So wherein did the devil's helmets come from?

There were no horns on the helmets in the town - but the fantasy of the satan's headgear is still alive. There have been no horns at the helmets in the town - however

however, the parable of the satan's headgear remains walking properly.

The "fault" for the arrival of this myth is probably borne thru the theatre gown fashion designer Cami Emil Doepler, who preferred to draw the target market's interest along along with his feature wicker parent. He decided that a horned helmet is probably pleasant for this cause and placed his idea into exercising via developing the costumes for Wagner's opera Ring of the Nibelung in 1876. Apparently, Doepler's imaginative and prescient turned into so top that it took root in the popularity of mass tradition audiences. No marvel, in any case, it suits perfectly into these people's meant "devilishness".

But it without a doubt is no longer the quality idea on the problem. According to each other speculation, the function helmet changed into presupposed to be a replica of Odin's photograph with ravens sitting on his shoulders: Hugina and Munina. The birds flew spherical the area each day to build up the current facts after which passed it straight away to the ear of the god.

Meanwhile, the helmets simply from the Viking tour length don't have any horns. They are rather easy headgear with an eye fixed shield and no decorations. The horned helmets on show in a few museums date returned to an in advance length - the Iron Age - and have been in all likelihood used in the path of the rite, not in war.

Today, mass way of life is slowly giving up cultivating this delusion. While in not very intense productions, the Vikings are humorously portrayed with horns on their heads, in those greater devoted recollections, this detail isn't placed. Horned helmets are therefore absent from the contemporary series approximately Northern warriors, or from Bernard Cornwell's novel.

four. Their cruelty had no limits

This fantasy is also the give up end result of a battle amongst one-of-a-kind cultures - pagan and catholic. The Vikings have been a humans expert in war and often showed a unethical to aggression and cruelty. There were also conditions after they tortured their sufferers. But did they in fact flow into a ways from the common for his or her era in this regard? I do no longer assume so

Contrary to typically repeated myths, the Vikings were now not mainly merciless or eager to combat - or as a minimum they have been no longer a ways from the common on this. It must be remembered that at that point the complete of Europe was beaten through smaller and larger wars, and blood turned into spilling in streams in almost every corner of Europe. The rulers needed to deal with their fighters definitively with the intention to maintain their positions. So the combat to the death and to existence became simply a way of looking after one's very own interests. And the Vikings were humans tailor-made to the times wherein they lived. The simplest difference have become their unfamiliarity with the idea of holiness: for the invaders from the North, a monastery or church have grow to be similar to the relaxation of the constructing full of loot, and priests were easy opponents.

Moreover, the method to other cultures at that point became definitely particular from that of today. When Scandinavian warriors contacted the human beings of France or England, they were frequently labeled as "stupid barbarians". Therefore, their cultural identification remained fantastic from that of Europe, and this modified into contemplated inside the hiccups of the Vikings' enemies inside the route of intervals of pillaging. As Robert Fergusson writes:

The psychopathic fury of the invaders, marked with the aid of the identical inhuman indifference to the sufferers that characterised Charlemagne in the direction of the Saxons, positioned vent within the childish brutality of transgressive behaviour, presenting the satisfaction of breaking taboos in their private and their patients. Simeon of Durham cited that the attackers deliberately drowned the clergymen inside the sea; it is viable that this changed into a few form of merciless parody of baptism.

five. They averted bathing

Today, the wicker is frequently visible as a dirty, sweaty and sea-winded big, for whom number one hygiene guidelines are restrained to unintended bathing within the sea. Meanwhile, the fact grow to be diametrically actually one in every of a type.

Archaeological research discovered out that the medieval people of the North used crests, tweezers and razors on a everyday foundation. What is greater, they took excellent care in their hairstyle and cautious beard styling. John of Wallingford wrote within the thirteenth century about wikings as: "the heartbreakers of the unknowns". Surely stinking, baggy men would not were so a success. And that isn't always all! The word "Saturday" in Old Scandinavian technique certainly "laundry day", which at least indicates a high first-class take care of garments (and toward the records of Europe on the time, laundry as quickly as each week changed into nonetheless the height of hygiene).

So the Vikings sincerely had to shine in evaluation with different cultures, which is likewise evidenced through the fashion for his or her hairstyles, costumes and artwork that got here on the court docket docket of King Ethelred, who reigned in England at the flip of the ninth and tenth centuries. As the pupil Alkuin wrote to the king: "Look at those superfluous robes, hairstyles, manners. You see the resemblance to pagan hairstyles and fords? Aren't the people you need to mimic the equal barbarians who oppress us?"

Chapter 11: Torture Some Of The Vikings

The entire of England and France lived in worry in their brutality. Viking tortures have grown to be an infamous photograph of pagan bestiality. A bloody eagle, gutting enemies But what is the reality approximately Viking torture? And which of them had been the worst?

One aspect's for sure: the black legend have come to be earlier of the soldiers of the North, anywhere they went. The stories about the torture and homicide fairs that the Vikings used to set up for themselves in the course of their war expeditions delivered about such worry a number of the populace of Christian Europe that they frequently just ran away on the sight of feature ships. Even Charlemagne, hearing approximately the fleet drawing near the borders of his america, come to be supposed - in keeping with biographers - to be in tears. What had been they so terrified of?

The most drastic torture (and on the equal time the method of execution), which nowadays is attributed to the Vikings, changed into the so-called "bloody eagle". The originator of this ritualistic method of killing the sufferer need to were endowed with a really sadistic imagination. The lowering out of the eagle consisted in Cutting out the ribs from the once more with an axe, and then dragging them outside. The very last "decoration" modified into the wretched lungs, that have been free at the open chest to resemble wings.

It come to be with this approach, in line with the descriptions of numerous authors of the sagas approximately the human beings of the North, that Ivar's father Without Bones come to be to avenge the dying of his father. Skald Sigvat stated in his poem dated 1030: "Ivar, who resided in York, lessen an eagle at the decrease returned of Aella [from Nortombria]", which come to be later picked up thru successive biographers and poets. The "Orkney Saga" of 1200 already includes a whole description of the ritual, completed not by using way of the use of Ivar himself, however additionally via manner of various Vikings.

This does not recommend, but, that they immortalized the image of the proud bird furthermore on the bodies in their enemies. Contemporary historians typically typically generally tend to agree that this kind of torture couldn't be used frequently. Why? First of all, the sufferer might have died from bloodshed inside the early ranges, lengthy before the "ornament" have become finished. Secondly, it is very probably that the complete story end up simply made up!

Researchers anticipate that Sigvat can also additionally have in truth used the metaphor of an eagle attacking a prey (the chook could of course be Ivar, and the hunted might be Aella). What about the scenes engraved on stone with the resource of Stora Hammars of Gotland, that have extended been interpreted as proof of this drastic torture? Already within the Eighties, the medical press have become essential of this speculation. A historian from Yale University, Roberta Frank, argued, for example, that the younger the payments of the executions, the extra brutal they are.

It is consequently feasible that the "bloody eagle" modified into most effective a bullshit invented with the useful resource of using Christians, due to lousy translation and panicky fear. According to the competitive idea of predation, the fowl of prey turn out to be not cut out however drawn on the decrease back of the defeated opponent to show its domination. But the truth that Victorian torture, the most famous torture in Victorian facts, have become out to be a misinterpretation does not suggest that warriors from the North did not understand and used certainly one of a type drastic techniques...

King Edmund and the Torture Tree

Also on this manner of pasturing the enemy, the precept protagonist (or rather: the executioner) have turn out to be Ivar, who was often referred to as "the maximum brutal of all of the leaders of the city". In 870, after defeating King Edmund's navy inside the East of England, he preferred the captured European ruler to give up his religion. He ordered his warriors to tie him to a tree and flog him. When this did not help - Edmund modified into meant to call on Christ all of the time, which does not appear particularly extraordinary in this type of state of affairs - the monarch modified into thrown down with stones and then treated as a taking pictures guard. Eventually the resigned Ivar had the victim reduce down.

The story of Edmund's execution spread quick throughout Europe. And based totally on the ones testimonies, among 985 and 987, more than a century later, a biography of the ruler become created. By that point the descriptions of the Vikings' cruelty had already taken on a completely exalted person. They were accused, for example, of deliberately recreating the martyrdom of the crucified Christ and St. Sebastian, who died with arrows.

The hassle is that the human beings of the North at that point couldn't apprehend the Christian saints, so notwithstanding the truth that the resemblance in fact existed, it modified into completely at random. The writer of Passio Sancti Eadmundi, Abbo of Fleury, moreover wrote that after being flogged the pores and pores and skin on the king's another time cracked and the ribs have come to be seen, which in turn resembled a "bloody eagle", so we already have a full set of atrocities Apparently the galloping creativeness, fear and the passage of time accomplished a substantial function here all yet again. As the unlucky ruler definitely did, we probably will in no way find out once more.

The tree as a relevant element of torture and execution regarded inside the case of some other approach - gutting, which is likewise taken into consideration by means of way of the Vikings to be a well-known way of causing lack of life. According to the Saga of Nyal written in the thirteenth century after the Battle of Clontarf in 1014, the Apache of Brodir and his people were captured. The torturer modified into the already "transformed" warrior Ulf the Restless. He ripped the belly of Brodir, and then rushed him throughout the trunk till all of the guts had been outdoor (amazing then the sufferer become to die).

The whole story can be very perverse. On the only hand, we have a Viking Christian killing a Viking pagan, who also rejected Christianity after being ordained. On the opposite hand, the very way of execution resembles a sacrificial ritual, worshipping the god Odin. So what emerge as Ulf's true aim at the equal time as he decided a way to punish an apostate? Here, too, historians can simplest speculate...

A snake into the godless

Olaf I Tryggvason - like Ulf - turned into a top notch supporter of Christianity and determined to introduce a ultra-contemporary faith via pressure. It isn't always tough to bet that the king's subversive concept got here up in the direction of difficult resistance in Norway. The truth that Olaf locked eighty Gentiles inside the temple at the very beginning of his campaign and burned them alive have grow to be in reality no longer beneficial in calming the battle.

Rauda of Salten additionally found out how merciless he turn out to be inside the course of folks who resisted Christianization. He promised him "the worst feasible demise" if he did now not receive Christ's teachings.

After some unique refusal, he ordered Raud to put a bit of timber among his enamel, and then attempted to push a venomous snake into the mouth of the sufferer.

As the poet and historian Snorri Sturlson stated, the clever Norwegian blew at the animal, so the method failed. Then Olaf slipped a department of angelica into Raud's throat and allow the reptile in via it, furthermore rushing it with warm iron.

Olaf I Tryggvason christianized his human beings with the resource of stress. And he did now not hesitate to use torture for this purpose.

As to the very last impact of the execution, you may make numerous guesses. Snorri wrote that the snake "crawled into Raud's mouth and deep into his throat till it hollowed out the exit in his facet and Raud have become finished". However, this appears as an possibility no longer going. If a sufficiently thick snake had really gotten deep into his mouth, the victim could certainly suffocate.

A probable worried reptile ought to have bitten Raud; the impact would possibly then depend upon the species of snake. Naturally, there was then a zigzag viper at the Scandinavian Peninsula, but it's miles feasible that the Norwegian king had a more amazing "device" of execution at his disposal. It is also viable that the whole state of affairs have become made up, and the scene of Raud and the god of the spirit accountable snake became an allegory of Christianizing terror that brought Olaf to Scandinavia.

Brutal Performances?

When numerous cultures, with their deeply rooted traditions and rituals, come into contact with every awesome, frequently exaggeration and misrepresentation takes place. This is the basis for the legends that later upward thrust up - which incorporates the ones created even as Christians from Europe "met" the peoples of the North.

The Vikings did now not understand the idea of holiness; they handled monasteries as easy targets full of valuable loot. That is why the authors of texts from those instances (particularly Christians) gave them very darkish capabilities. Meanwhile, most of the sufferers of the Scandinavian invaders died absolutely "as a popular" - in the course of fight or because of tough situations in captivity.

It is, but, distinctly clean to hint the path of notion of an observer of non secular rituals, who from the monastery modified into sent the various Vikings. The population of the North, for instance, had the dependancy of nailing useless animals committed to the gods to the timber. As Adam Bremenski wrote in the 11th century, the pagans made an supplying of male animals within the holy grove - one of each species, together with a horse, a dog or even a person.

From the material from Oserberg it's far concluded that the Vikings additionally preferred to cling their offerings. It become a weird tribute to Odin, the patron saint of hangers, who had the capability to talk to the lifeless. Snorri moreover mentions a completely unique shape of ritual geared in the direction of taming the deities, together with a "faux" sacrifice from the chief. When no prayers helped at some point of a hard time, the community ruler became "hung" on a rope from a calf's gut and "pierced" with reed through using a clergyman.

Since the peoples of the North have resorted to such representations of their war for survival, it's miles greater than probably that maximum of the legends about their beastlyness wereMade up. And as for the torture itself, it virtually gave way in each manner to that used by the Christian Inquisition fast afterwards.

Chapter 12: Viking Crimes

They may upward thrust out of the ocean like demons, destroy, rob and homicide, after which disappear with their loot, leaving the ruins at the back of. "From the fury of the humans of the North, maintain us, Lord," they begged with fear. But God did no longer usually listen to prayers

"It's been almost 350 years due to the fact we and our ancestors inhabited this lovable island, and there has in no manner been this form of horror in Britain as we have got now professional at the fingers of the pagan race, nor turn out to be it even perception that such an attack from the ocean may additionally want to arise." - wrote Alkuin, a pupil and a monk living in Frank lands to King Etelred of Nortombria. "Look at St. Kutbert's church, splashed with the blood of God's clergymen, robbed to shreds with its embellishes, the maximum honorable region of all in all of Britain has been spent at the pasture of pagan peoples."

Alkuin in his letters of direction refers to the assault on Lindisfarne in 793. This have come to be one of the most famous acts of violence perpetrated by using the use of the Vikings, whom the monk at once calls "wolves. This brutal attack became all the more surprising as it changed into there that the heart of Christian Nortombria changed into beating, wherein Kutbert, who died in an air of mystery of holiness in 687, have become a bishop and wherein his remains rested.

The Vikings have already written down the statistics of the British Isles on the stop of the 8th century. In the Chronicle of the Anglo-Saxons we have a look at that a set of Normans landed on the island of Portland in Dorset, wherein they had been taken as customers and asked to pay the toll. The wretched guy, who attributed ideal intentions to them, becomes manifestly killed. According to the chronicler's account, at the beginning "the pagans invaded and destroyed the British shoreline", and with time they began out to move inland frequently.

In 802 and 806 they attacked a wealthy abbey on the island of Iona, with the second raid being so fatal that the few surviving monks ultimately wanted to leave the island and circulate the abbey to Kells. However, Prior Blathmac MacFlainn and some of his brothers stayed there. They have been prepared to die in defence of the holy location - and did not need to attend extended for that. They were lessen into a trunk, and the sooner have been tortured. According to the define of German abbot Reichenau:

The cursed wild bunch rushed through the buildings, threatening quite blessed guys, and having murdered the rest of the community with furious cruelty, they became to the holy father to strain him to release the precious metals, among which lie the bones of Saint Columbus [] however the holy guy, without a gun in his arms, saved his will steadfast, used to stand as a whole lot as his enemies.

A yr later, the Vikings burned down severa abbeys in Galway Bay (alongside side Inishmurray and Roscam), and in 821 Howth in Dublin County become "looted via pagans who captured a big variety of girls. Several years later fleets of invaders from the North, each with 60 boats, ravaged the Cos Meath and Kildare valleys. The description of Leinster Maelciarain's chieftain's loss of life in 869 says that he have become betrayed with the aid of the usage of his humans and handed over to the Normans, who chopped him up after which used the severed head as a firing squad. This event is recorded inside the so-referred to as Three Chronicles of Ireland.

It wasn't any higher on the continent. In the French Brothers' Yearbooks in 842, Bishop Prudentius of Troyes defined how "the Norman fleet attacked the agreement of

Quentovic at dawn, plundered it and razed it to the ground, enslaving or massacring the two sexes". Emphasizing that women (and probably youngsters) had been moreover sufferers of the invaders come to be then a common way of showing the bestiality of the human beings of the North.

Under the 365 days 843 we take a look at in turn that during Nantes the Vikings "killed the bishop and hundreds of priests, both sexes, and plundered the town". Several times the chronicler factors out that the atrocities of the freshmen from across the ocean had been severa. In a similar tone he spoke approximately the ever present terror of the Normans dwelling inside the center of the 9th century Hermitage of Noirmoutier, the abbot of Saint-Philibert de Tournus in Burgundy and the author of the chronicle De translationibus et miraculis sancti Filiberti. In this chronicle he described more than one Viking raids on his monastery:

The type of ships is developing, the in no manner-finishing inflow of the Vikings will growth unstoppable. Everywhere Christ's humans fall victim to slaughter, hearth and looting. The Vikings flood the whole lot in their route and no character is able to oppose them []. Countless ships are crusing up the Seine and within the entire place evil is growing in energy. The Rouen has been ravaged, looted and burned. Paris, Beauvais and Meaux taken, the citadel in Melun razed to the floor, Chartres occupied, Evreux and Bayeux plundered, and each town closed in the lap.

As time went through, the invaders grew bolder and bolder inland, until in 845 they sailed up the Seine and, beneath Ragnar's control, stormed Paris. At the same time, the first Viking assault on the Iberian Peninsula befell. The invaders were led thru way of Bjorn Ironfoot and Hasting, who've been described within the Arabic chronicles as "merciless people not but seen in our u. S.".

The Arab chronicler Al-Nuwayri, living on the turn of the 13th and 14th centuries, wrote that the murderous Vikings, plundering Seville in 844, "did not even spare the draught animals. Duald Mac Fuirbis, however, mentioned that "they added with them to Ireland a brilliant range of Moorish prisoners for a long time these blue human beings have been in Ireland". At the equal time, for the duration of this period, William the Conqueror, Roll's superb-grandson or Rolf, the primary ruler of Normandy, changed the information of Europe with the aid of taking up the power within the u . S . A ., which his ancestors so willingly invaded and plundered.

Simeon of Durhan, who is credited with the Regum Story, describes the Vikings with animal metaphors, such as "stinging hornets" and "bloodthirsty wolves", on the equal time as attributing to them the worst crimes. "By ruthlessly snatching, they've got grew to grow to be everything proper into a drumstick, trampled holy objects with their holy ft, dug up altars and pillaged all the church treasures," he says. "They killed some of the brethren, tied some shamefully and abandoned others bare, and drowned others inside the sea.

In the face of such own family individuals, it isn't sudden that there was a consistent threat of a Vilnius invasion additionally the various woman population of the convents. According to the legend of St. Ebba, the Prior of Coldingham, in worry of the upcoming Danes, reduce off her nose and top lip and endorsed the nuns to do the same. In this manner they had been to avoid shame.

Many medieval chroniclers shared the hatred of the terrifying Vikings. Adam of Bremen, describing the Viking invasion of

Frank lands in 882, says that they "made amusing of our humans. In flip, Henry of Huntington, in his History of Anglorum, describes the website online web page visitors from the North as "swarms of bees, the cruellest of parents that don't spare every person due to their age or gender". Also Florence of Worcester remembers the severa crimes dedicated through Sven, who invaded Mercy in 1013, committing "more than one acts of barbarism".

The Europeans residing at the coasts seemed to the sea in fear of the invaders from the North.

Photo: Nicholas Roerich/Public Domain Europeans residing at the coasts appeared to the sea in fear of the invaders from the North.

This "lightness" in killing and torturing Christians, specifically monks, stunned historians most. In the Anglo-Saxon Chronicle we observe that during the plundering of Cantenbury in 1011 Archbishop Elfeg (the chronicler erroneously offers the name Duncan) become taken prisoner thru the Vikings, whose wild fats tormented him for no longer trying to pay the invaders. An account of this occasion may be determined inside the Thietmar Chronicle:

A crowd of pagans surrounded him and he changed into carrying guns of a sizeable variety to take his life. When their leader Thurkil observed it from afar, he ran speedy and so he referred to as out: "I beg you, do now not do this! I will gladly provide you with all gold and silver, and some factor I private or gather in any way, besides my deliver, so you do no longer commit against the law on God's anointing. But the wrath of his companions, extra difficult than iron and rock, became no longer softened with the beneficial useful resource of his human speech; it modified into not till the blood of the innocent shed that he have grow to be satisfied, that he was proper away attracted to it by way of the preference of the skulls, the hail of stones and wood bullets.

Even earlier than Knut or Sven, Ivar Boneless come to be the chief in cruelty. Today it's miles now not feasible to mention whether or not or now not he modified into in reality sick or whether or now not the nickname had a one-of-a-kind, greater metaphorical that means, however he come to be supposedly an exceedingly cruel guy. He is credited, among one of a kind subjects, with the murder of St. Edmund, King of East England, whom he ordered to be tortured and then killed by using beheading.

The king of Nortumbria Ælla, who, consistent with legend, killed Ivar's father, the well-known Ragnar Lodbrok, with the useful resource of using throwing him right into a pit complete of snakes, did not get maintain of the grace of holiness. According to the legend, the vengeful Ivar had him killed in 867 with an exceedingly modern torture - decreasing out a so-called bloody eagle on his lower lower back. In 873, at the identical time because the merciless ruler died, he became stated in the Ulster Yearbooks as "king of all the Scandinavians in Ireland and Britain," the chief of a "first rate pagan navy" that were conquering Anglo-Saxon kingdoms and taking on the land for over a decade.

The Battle of Stamford Bridge in 1066 is regularly considered to be the prevent of the invasions to Great Britain in Victoria.

Photo: Peter Nicolai Arbo/ Public Domain
The Battle of Stamford Bridge in 1066 is

frequently taken into consideration to be the cease of the invasions to Great Britain.

Medieval European citizens had been afraid to look prolonged boats carrying loss of life and destruction. The human beings of the international locations invaded via the use of way of the Normans observed them as barbaric monsters who, like a punishment from heaven, fell on their heads, murdered, enslaved and robbed, and what they couldn't rob, they became a drummer. They had been strangers to mercy, pity, worry of God; they committed crimes incomprehensible to medieval Christians.

Were they really such monsters? If we bear in mind that Charlemagne murdered four,500 pagan Saxons in 782 for rise up towards tries to impose Christianity on them, and furthermore do not forget the recognition of murders of clergy or mutilations of circle of relatives in the households of Christian rulers of the generation, the Vikings do not seem so terrible. Perhaps it is immoderate time to unfasten the nasty patch of cruel beasts?

Drink like a real Viking

Thor, Loki, and the bet approximately having a corner with beer? Under the eye of the without cease drunken Odin, it changed into possible. And the Vikings have been sure to in shape their gods in consuming.

Because the wine itself is a effective god

Odin is normally alive.

Odin hasn't been eating something but wine. More, he did no longer take something in his mouth but wine. He did no longer eat something. Nothing for a chew of the bolt. Not even a sawmill. Edda Elder leaves no doubt about it.

It can also moreover seem outstanding that a Scandinavian deity would now not see the vicinity beyond wine whilst it's not a completely well-known Scandinavian product. But it truly is the element. Wine emerge as the most luxurious drink within the accumulate of a rich wicker. It could have come from Germany or perhaps France, imported from the stays of the Roman Empire. The wine becomes a status photo, so Odin, the No. 1 Viking pantheon god, needed to have it in any respect charges. The king of the gods could not drink beer; it would not look like lots.

It can also seem similarly abnormal that Odin failed to consume some thing. Wine on an empty belly harms. This type of a diet plan pulled for eternity can havoc the gastrointestinal tract and is positive to be powerful in insanity. The reality that Odin drank terrific wine in all likelihood makes his call honestly recommend "loopy".

Some human beings provide an reason at the back of it as "ecstatic", however frankly talking, and given his ingesting conduct, "Odin" certainly manner beneath the have an effect on of alcohol.

It's an intensive exchange. Most polytheistic religions have one boss god, in addition to a piece of a aspect god of drunkenness/wine/beer face and so forth. Enlil emerge as higher than Ninkasi; Amon to Hathor, Zeus to Dionysus. The god of drunkenness comes, brings fun and confusion, and however is normally difficulty to wiser customs and higher energy of the chief god, who commonly has a beard. It does no longer take the sharpest theologian to parent out why. Drunkenness needed to find a niche within society, a nook in which it could be tamed and managed.

But in the Vikings, the precept god is a drunken god. He even has the decision "under the affect of alcohol." The Vikings had no unique alcohol god. It grow to be Odin. And that is because of the truth alcohol and drunkenness did not want to find out an area inside the community, they created that community. Alcohol have turn out to be energy, own family, records, poetry, army provider and future.

Being an abstinent Viking must were a dwarfing undertaking and there has been no trace left of such an man or woman residing.

There is some thing to be said approximately the varieties of percentage beverages absorbed through the Vikings. There have been quality 3. The above cited wine, which, because it has been said, price a fortune, so it become beyond the gain of virtually anyone. Hierarchically, the following drink changed into honey, drinkable, candy and pretty expensive. Almost every person almost continuously pulled a beer. The Viking brogue in all likelihood had a bit more strength than ours, approximately eight percentage, and as excavations display, it changed into dark and malty.

But in Viking sagas, all heroes drink honey, due to the truth honey modified into beauty France. That's why while you wanted to demonstrate which you had been a real pansy, you have got been building a honeymoon, although its walls smelled now not some thing however beer. But notwithstanding the fact that, for the sake of appearances, it turned into referred to as a honeymoon. It may want to best be the size of a medium room - a few have been 3.Five meters by using 5. They had been massive, nearly one hundred meters lengthy. When Hrothgar desires to emerge as a effective king in Beowulf, he builds Heorot, the largest honeymoon room the world has seen, complete of pillars and gold.

If you have got had been given a honeymoon, you've got a whole mouth, because of the truth your first duty is to supply the liquor to the infantrymen, so when you have a honeymoon, you have got someone to location the honey to. That's the way you confirmed yourself in your lordhood in a clear and legible way.

And vice versa, whilst you went to drink honey in his honeymoon, the honour ordered to protect the founder with arms. Alcohol changed into energy. Literally. He made human beings swear their loyalty. A king with out a honeymoon have become like a banker without coins or a library without books.

The queen could not be missing both, due to the fact however the fact that it can seem uncommon, ladies had been a in reality essential part of the feast inside the honeymoon. The ladies - or the snacks of peace inside the Viking nomenclature - saved an eye constant on the order of the night meal, soothed the turbulent environment and provided a healthful dose of lady peace. They had been accountable for sumbl logistics, which in Nordic meant a drunken dinner party. Perhaps they even cherished the preliminary moments of the night time, when the first queues have been devoted to Odin (for victory), Njord and Freya (for peace and outstanding harvest), and then they drank minnisöl, a beer of reminiscence, in honour of the spirits of their ancestors and useless buddies.

She poured honey (or beer) through a small sieve, which she wore on a series spherical her neck. It grow to be also the instantaneous while she ought to provide him public advice ceremonially. This became probably quite simple, e.G. "drink", but there were moreover real statements. Once the king drank, the queen served all his warriors, from the most critical to the least vital, and at the surrender she served the drink to the traffic.

To inform the fact, in Viking poetry, the vicinity of a girl modified into to serve drinks. In poetry, a lady end up not referred to as a lady, she changed into referred to as serving liquor. There is a thirteenth-century textbook for a amateur bard. According to it:

A female need to be described through the phrases taken from all styles of unbeauty, gold and gemstones, in addition to beer, wine and other liquids which she pours or serves; in addition, with the phrases for beer dishes and additionally for everything that is proper for her to do or deliver.

So a woman can be called a pouring beer, a honeymooner or a liquor charmer, due to the fact in the idea of the Vikings, who had been no longer well-known for his or her fancy, could not be some thing and now not something else. This abuse of the outer edge turned into because of the fact that the Vikings may additionally additionally want to in no way call topics by means of way of their first name. All their poetry is constructed in the course of the precept that one need to invent indistinct phrases for commonly diagnosed subjects. So the ocean have come to be referred to as the whale drink, the kingdom of crabs or the frothy beer of the coast. Blood modified right into a warmness wolf's sap, hearth grow to be the destruction of the house, and heaven turned into the burden of dwarves. This is what makes Viking poetry so pleasantly incomprehensible.

That's additionally why you drink honey from hrimkaldars, frosted cups, due to the fact in fact, the Vikings drank from glass vessels. Not all of us - glass have become luxurious, however the king in his honeymoon likely had a glass that appeared no particular than those we use these days. There had been remarkable shapes, sizes and colors. Most could possibly look pretty ordinary on modern-day table, despite the fact that possibly a bit kitschy. You in all likelihood had a tough approach if you imagined that all the Vikings were ingesting from hollow skulls and horns.

There is a funny sort of frosted Viking cup that archaeologists call a funnel cup. But this is because of the reality archaeologists do now not have a poetic nature. The funnel cup is about 12 cm tall and is precisely the shape you can don't forget, because of this it can't be located on the desk. It would possibly honestly wobble. There is a motive for this, as it's all about swallowing everything at once. The Vikings linked awesome significance to this, because of the reality when you hit the chalice straight away, you could see which you were a actual guy. This changed into moreover the cause of the greater traditional consuming right away; the delicatessen's masculinity changed into examined through checking his functionality to swallow huge doses of intoxicating fluids as an entire.

There is a story about Thor (god of warfare and hammers) and Loki (god of nasty numbers). Loki challenged Thor, claiming that he could not drink a corner of beer. Thor, who had by no means been able to face up to the challenge, standard it, and Loki had the nook added to the desk and said a real guy would possibly drink it in a single fell swoop. Thor kidnapped the horn, placed it in his mouth and drank, and drank, and drank, and drank, but despite the fact that he from time to time have been given off, the horn become though nearly entire. Loki showed his unhappiness and stated that any common ancients could end the horn in sips. So Thor attempted once more, and all over again the divine eating have grow to be a waste. Loki purrred that any weakling might be able to drink the contents of the nook in three. The scenario repeats itself. Then Thor feels very embarrassed and discouraged until Loki famous that he led him into the sector and that he connected the corner to the sea. Thor drank a lot that he dwindled the level of the area's oceans, and so, in step with the Vikings, tides were created.

Apart from the opposition of drunkenness, the Vikings have been boasting. There become no longer anything incorrect with that. The Viking changed into expected to boast. That he'd speak about all his dandruffy jumps. Then some other Viking have turn out to be speculated to beat him. Unfortunately, there have been no modest Vikings, shy Normans, clumsy rapists and embarrassing dandruffers off the English coast. They favored to yell out what that they had achieved, bragging and claiming to have demonstrated greater in terms of rape and looting than their colleague next door.

And those boasting of them were now not compact vouchers. They were streams of speak talkative whirlpools and lyrical tsunamis. These had been first rate, formalised events, just like modern rapper fights, at the least that's what I'm reporting. Moreover, all the boasting come to be taken deadly severely. It come to be predicted that the boaster might no longer deny something he boasted approximately, whether or not or not it become about the past or truly planned. One could not excuse oneself the subsequent morning as we would have completed, explaining that it became really gibberish over a pitcher. No, no, it became exactly the alternative. They used a completely unique cup, bragarfull, a promise cup. When you swore to do some component and shaved from that tumbler, the promise have end up one hundred% binding. You could not escape with it. Bragarfull = destiny.

To ensure that bragarfull may need to not be retracted, one turned into dragged to the corridor of the holy boar and swore on him, putting his hand on the bristles. Then the animal modified into slaughtered, his spirit flew to the goddess Frei and suggested the drunken oath.

There is a tale about a person named Hethin. When during a night meal at the king's residence there has been a bragarfull, Hethin hit him, patted the boar, and broke out the announcement that he could marry his sister-in-regulation. The next day he turn out to be damn silly, truely all and sundry is probably, so he went to his brother and confessed what he changed into doing. The reaction of the fascinated birthday celebration came right all the way down to phrases: "Well, bragarfull is bragarfull, so you gotta get to paintings rapid."

Perhaps this can further improve your records of the fee of women inside the Viking community. But that a few days later your brother died in an accidental duel, the whole lot ended happily.

All of this as a minimum partially explains why ladies have been referred to as the spinners of peace and why peace had to be spinned, how a whole lot it got here in. It have become an exceptionally adventurous society, halls complete of warriors compelled to drink too much too quick, boast, because the ceremonial required, insult each wonderful and all carried swords. The sum of that is first-class expressed through the epic of the Vikings and Anglo-Saxons, Boewulf, wherein the poet tries to provide an explanation for what a terrific guy Boewulf have emerge as. He is praised with out a clue, and the best reward comes right down to the reality that Boewulf "never killed a drunken pal.

This apparently must had been a first-rate success for a wicked guy - a trait of character so unique that it needed to be underlined within the poem.

On sumbl there have been moreover scalds and musicians growing a track as an awful lot breath of their throats. The Vikings had a deep-rooted conviction that poetry comes instantly from alcohol. As the information changed into, the gods had prolonged, prolonged within the beyond fought a battle among themselves. Eventually they made peace and to seal it, they decided to spit in a cauldron. Hm, it could seem normal and unhygienic to you, but it need to be cited that during many primitive cultures human beings chewed barley at the pulp they spat out, because of this beginning the beer making method.

Never thoughts; in any case, on the equal time because the cauldron emerge as complete of saliva, a man named Acidir, the wisest guy- god that ever emerged from spit, jumped out of it. Acidir changed into a generous soul, and wandering the earth, coaching the human race all attention, till he met filthy dwarfs who killed him and let his blood drain into the cauldron. Then they poured a few honey into it and so Odrörir, the Honey of Poetry, have turn out to be born.

Then the big seemed, stole Odrörir from the dwarf and took him to his mountain palace. Odyn heard about it and wanted to sip this honey. But unfortunately, Odrörir now stood within the large's citadel, day and night time time guarded through way of his daughter.

However, Odin had a amazing preference for honey, and it's miles truly extraordinary what this type of man can also want to do whilst he felt like ingesting. He dug into the citadel and slid in, taking the shape of a snake. This is how he reached the huge's daughter, whom he seduced with little notion. He promised her a wedding in trade for a honey drink. It may be a completely precise custom inside the Viking global: if a girl gave a person a completely unique drink, he needed to marry her. It isn't always smooth how popular this subculture changed into, as most couples were in fact related to their parents, but we have were given every other example that you in reality needed to take a sip of something percentage and become the founder's brother/warrior/husband.

But Odin modified into an regular pig. He banged a cauldron right now (not unusual), became an eagle and flew away with the Honey of Poetry in his belly. The giant observed it, right away turned into an eagle and threw himself right into a fierce eagle chase.

The chase become very even. When the alternative gods located that Odin modified into coming domestic in Asgard, they located up a vat to provide Odrörir an area to throw up. The huge have become proper there. Odin quilted and puked pure poetry into the vat. Just so He had been given so disturbing and had a lot poetic enthusiasm in him that a hint little bit of Honey Poetry shook his ass. From the honey that Odyn threw up, a handful of the great poets that lived and lived amongst people got here into being. What flew out of his ass contributed to the creation of a big wide variety of poems. And so one fantasy explains the begin of people with the statistics of Shakespeare and W.H. Davies.

Beer changed into the keystone of Viking existence. They committed it to Odin. It grow to be the goal of life, an perception for poets and warriors seeking out possibilities to homicide. In one of the heroic sagas, the king involves a selection to prevent the jealousy many of the two higher halves, maintaining the one who will deliver him a higher beer whilst he returns from battle.

The honey room within the morning turn out to be likely one huge pigsty. There had been simplest elements missing. After extensive eating, vomiting and mating generally arise (preferably now not simultaneously). In the ancient Egyptians the entirety came all of the manner all the way all the way down to this. But the Vikings, irrespective of how many horns with honey/beer, in no way aspect out every of them. They did now not vomit, they did not mate. They had been asleep.

There is this sort of charming, legendary creature, the Heron of Frost (I don't have any concept why the Heron), that is said to have been rushing from the heavens within the course of the sumbl, and to have floated within the air until really anyone fell asleep. No one became coming home. One stayed in the nobleman's honey room until the eyelids fell down on their very non-public, fell on a bench or desk and proper away fell asleep in a stone dream. It emerges as a piece risky. All the infantrymen had been below the have an effect on of alcohol to the element of unconsciousness and defenceless like babies. A piece of Boewulf's poem tells the tale of ways a certain monster slipped into the honey room at night time until the hero, in a flash of intelligence, below the impact of alcohol to unconsciousness.

Honesty dictates that the hazard of being eaten by using the monster have turn out to be statistically negligible, however not being burned alive. It is stated that in the eighth century King Ingjald lived in Sweden, who invited all his kings' neighbours to his coronation. When it came to bragarfull, he swore to increase the dominion by means of manner of 1/2 in each course. Everyone have grow to be ingesting. Everybody have been given drunk. The Heron of Frost did herald's sleepwalking and even as everybody modified into asleep, Ingjald went out, locked the door and burned his honey room with all of the invited kings internal.

I would like to mention that the feat became a one-off, but I ought to lie. A lot of testimonies of burned honeymoon halls with human contents indoors survived. Even one queen reduce this range out of her companion just so justice might be finished.

But while you have got been a Viking, becoming a dull Viking wasn't so terrible. The Vikings have been obsessed with the vision of dying. They actually landed in Walhalla, in which there was an eternal balancing, sumbl after the end of time. There emerge as Odin, loopy from wine, there had been all the vintage buddies you used to drink beer to recollect, and there has been Heidrun, the divine goat, whose udders were always gushing with super, robust honey.